A LIFE IN BALANCE

Other books by Meg Wolff:

Becoming Whole:
The Story of My Complete Recovery from Breast Cancer

Breast Cancer Exposed:
The Connection Between Food and Survival

a life in balance

delicious, plant-based recipes
for optimal health

by
MEG WOLFF

foreword by
T. Colin Campbell, Ph.D.

preface by
Joan Benoit Samuelson

Down East

ISBN 978-0-89272-906-7

Cover design by Miroslaw Jurek
Interior design by Lynda Chilton

Front cover photograph by Russell French
Author photograph by Patricia McCarthy

Sandy Pukel's recipe for "Arame Stuffed Mushrooms" originally appeared in Sandy Pukel and
Mark Hanna's *Grains and Greens on the Deep Blue Sea*, published by Square One Publishers
(2007). It is republished here with permission from Sandy Pukel and Square One Publishers.

Kathy Freston's recipe for "Old Bay Tofu Cakes with Cream Horseradish and Creole Mustard
Sauce Over Shaved Fennel Slaw" is a creation from chef Tal Ronnen. It is reprinted here with
permission from Kathy Freston and Tal Ronnen.

Library of Congress Cataloging-in-Publication Data available on request

Printed in the United States of America

5   4   3   2

BOOKS·MAGAZINE·ONLINE
www.downeast.com

Distributed to the trade by National Book Network

I dedicate this book
to everyone who is making
an effort to eat
in a more deliciously
healthy way.

∾

20 PERCENT OF THE PROFITS FROM A LIFE IN BALANCE: DELICIOUS, PLANT-BASED RECIPES FOR OPTIMAL HEALTH WILL BE DONATED TO SHARE OUR STRENGTH, A NON-PROFIT ORGANIZATION THAT WORKS LOCALLY AND GLOBALLY TO HELP END CHILDHOOD HUNGER.

contents

foreword

T. Colin Campbell, Ph.D., is the world's foremost authority on plant-based diets. He's conducted more than forty years' worth of research on the subject.

His landmark book, The China Study, Startling Implications for Diet, Weight Loss and Long-Term Health, *is the single-most influential book I've ever read. When I first read it in 2005, I was amazed by how Dr. Campbell, a nutritional biochemist at Cornell, had spent his life doing scientific research about plant-based diets. I'd been eating that way since 1999, and was reassured to learn that it is, in fact, the healthiest way to eat, to maintain good health and prevent, and possibly even reverse, many of the degenerative diseases that plague our modern society.*

I wanted to ask Dr. Campbell to write the foreword to my first book, Becoming Whole: The Story of My Complete Recovery from Breast Cancer, *and for a year, I tried various ways of connecting with him. Then, sitting on my bed, re-reading* The China Study *(honest) on New Year's Day 2007, the phone rang. It was Dr. Campbell, thanking me for my persistence, and agreeing to write my foreword! I was so grateful then, and I am again now.*

Of the many questions I hear from those who hear my lectures or read our book, *The China Study,* on the evidence for a whole-food, plant-based dietary lifestyle, one of the most common is "What do I eat now?" And then, "What does this kind of diet look like?" "How do I go about doing that?"

Now I have a really good way to answer these questions: "Read Meg Wolff's new book."

I am very much aware that, for many people, beginning a new lifestyle can be intimidating in so many ways, but when the change is made, the rewards of eating this way far outweigh the costs.

Meg's book tells a real-life example of the power of a plant-based diet, not only to prevent but also to reverse chronic disease. While many in the medical "establishment" may not support this strategy, I am nonetheless finding that more and more individual physicians and other primary healthcare providers are turning to this kind of nutrition as treatment for their patients. The idea that eating vegetables and fruits (almost all their parts) can do more than simply prevent future ailments and diseases is a very exciting concept. We now know that this same strategy can be used to treat ailments already present.

More and more people are willing to make drastic lifestyle changes in the name of better health. We are reaching a tipping point, and a critical mass of success stories like Meg's is accumulating.

Meg healed herself through a diet based on whole grains, beans, and vegetables, and a big dose of determination. The science behind eating this way made absolute sense to her and she ran with it, ultimately becoming living proof of the heavily researched idea that changing to a plant-based diet will improve your health.

Meg's is an excellent and personally inspiring story, and people want and need excellent examples. She's not the only example, but hers is as good as it gets. This all-important link between what we eat and our health is finally becoming understood... we're beginning to see such a hopeful turnaround of thinking in this country.

This great new cookbook from Meg—full of her own simple, delicious recipes and those from numerous celebrated contributors—has the potential to help millions of people better understand how easy it can be to make improvements in their diet. Her contributors range from Olympic athletes to medical doctors to suburban housewives to firefighters to NBA basketball stars—showing that ANYONE can make their lives better by improving their diet and making their best life even better. People resist making changes, but this book will help people to realize that it doesn't have to be daunting.

I appreciate Meg's approach. She is inclusive, and wants people to feel good about ANY good changes they make . . . and she doesn't expect anything from anyone . . . she encourages steps in the right direction and educates people along the way.

This book shows how easy it is to take positive steps to a healthier future. The recipes in this book are simple to prepare. They contain minimal or no added oil, sugar, and salt. Meg's approach is to use whole foods—foods unchanged from their natural state.

I can only wish Meg and all her readers of this book the very best as they participate in a much-needed healthcare revolution.

—T. Colin Campbell, Ph.D.
Jacob Gould Schurman Professor Emeritus of Nutritional Biochemistry, Cornell University
Co-author of *The China Study: Startling Implications for Diet, Weight Loss, and Long-Term Health*

preface

Of course, I first knew of Joan through her running and the Olympics. In 1998, when my kids attended Cape Elizabeth schools—which Joan did, too—I admired the statue of her in front of the town library.

I later met Joanie at a fund-raiser for breast cancer research. Later, my friend Dr. Lisa Belisle, Joanie, and I tossed around the idea of writing a cookbook together, but the timing just wasn't the best. My husband Tom, a longtime runner, also knows Joanie through his work with Nike and mutual running friends.

Joan is one of the most industrious, busy people I've ever encountered. She's a huge backer of Friends of Casco Bay, is the founder and chair of the annual world-class Beach to Beacon road race, and is involved in countless organizations and efforts. I'm proud to know her and have her be a part of my book.

It is with admiration and many shared interests that I applaud Meg and embrace her collection of healthy and tasty recipes included in this book. It delights me that so many of the recipes highlight ingredients that can be found close to home and heart, in home gardens or local farmers' markets.

Meg's myriad vegetables and grains in these recipes makes cooking an adventure and keeps the palate pleased.

As a mother, athlete, community volunteer, and gardener, I understand the importance of living a balanced life and eating a balanced diet in a way that also supports the local community and environment in a healthy and sustainable way.

I have long been an advocate of using good nutrition and regular exercise as a panacea for illness and as part of the protocol for recovery. They restore health to people challenged by cancer and other diseases as well as by lack of physical activity and good nutrition.

Meg uses her experience and passion for cooking and improving the habits and health of others in easy recipes that are presented in impressive, creative, and easy-to-follow ways.

Having been invited to dine with Meg at her home, I can assure you that you will find the recipes included in this book fulfilling in every way.

Cook, and run on!

—Joan Benoit Samuelson

introduction

Welcome to *A Life in Balance: Delicious, Plant-Based Recipes for Optimal Health* and congratulations! Your interest in this book shows you want to eat in a healthy way and keep your life in balance. That's excellent!

I hope my recipes will be appealing and inspiring, whether you're starting from an already healthy point or just turning a corner toward a healthier lifestyle.

You'll see that I like to keep it simple whenever possible. But that does *not* mean boring! When I ditched my junk-food-filled life in an effort to heal from invasive breast cancer in 1998, many people around me made comments about how sad it was that I'd have to eat bland food. That is *such* a misconception. The standard American diet that most people eat is actually very limited. I discovered a whole new, expansive, amazing world when I started eating healthier. It turns out there were thousands of things I had never tried, and there are still thousands more things to try. A burger and fries now hold no interest for me because what I eat is so much tastier—and far better for me.

This cheerful cookbook represents my effort to bring the benefits of eating healthy to light—and into the mainstream. I believe we're finally at the cusp of people "getting it"— the need to improve their diets, to make changes in how and what they eat, to have more energy, to be around for their kids, to be happier in general.

I've invited some well-respected friends to help me get this all-important message out: that what we eat really matters. I'm delighted to be able to share some of their healthy recipes. I know they'll reinforce the diet–health link!

I wrote *Becoming Whole: The Story of My Complete Recovery from Breast Cancer* after surviving both bone cancer and then breast cancer. Doctors had given me essentially no hope of long-term survival after I underwent a mastectomy (after having had my leg amputated eight years earlier), chemotherapy, and radiation. Nothing got better for me until I dramatically improved my diet. Paying attention to what I was eating transformed everything about my life. I couldn't go through such an experience and not share what I had learned.

Becoming Whole is the all-in-one book that I wish had existed as I was on my journey back to good health. It tells my story, but it's also a how-to manual that explains the science behind a plant-based diet, and it contains a wealth of resources and plant-based recipes. I wanted readers—most of whom are being told day to day about how *little control* you have over obstacles—to understand that there is so much *you can do* to make things better in the face of a medical crisis. First and foremost is improving the way you eat.

A Life in Balance: Delicious, Plant-Based Recipes for Optimal Health is the next logical step for me in getting my message out there. As I've maintained my health over the past twelve years, I've gradually expanded my diet. I started out eating a strict macrobiotic diet based primarily on grains, beans, and vegetables. I remain true to those basic concepts that I believe saved my life, and my diet is still centered around these healthy foods. I have, however, broadened what I eat, and the recipes in this new book reflect that expansion (I've included some good ol' standbys as well!)

I encourage you to remember that it only takes small steps to add up to better health over time. If you feel limited by your budget, don't worry about going completely organic. Do what you *can* do. Pat yourself on the back for buying some greens from a local farmers' market or the grocery store, or just serving up some healthy brown rice with toasted pumpkin seeds instead of cheesy noodles!

Beyond the recipes in this book, I've included lots of information and tips that I hope will help you stay focused on a healthy lifestyle. It's the most important thing you can do for yourself and your loved ones. I've learned this and I want to share that message with as many people as possible.

notes

Kombu is a sea vegetable, available at most health food stores. If you use it, great—kombu adds minerals and can help make beans easier to digest. But if you don't have it, it's not a show-stopper! Recipes in this book will work fine without it, too.

Water: Wherever water is called for in a recipe, I recommend using either spring water or filtered tap water to reduce the impurities in your food.

Soy sauce: When soy sauce is listed in a recipe, I recommend Eden or Mitoku brands. Aged 1 to 3 years is best.

Juice and Syrup: I recommend 100% pure, with no sugar or high-frutose corn syrup added.

Sea Vegetables: Where arame, wakame, kombu, or other nutrient-rich sea vegetables are listed, the amount is the dry measure. Reconstitute for 3 to 5 minutes.

grains

Whole Grains vs. Cracked Grains

Many Americans build their meals, especially dinner, around meat. My meals start with a grain. You might try this approach one or two nights a week at first, but make sure you add some vegetables, too! You've probably seen a lot of advertising about food products that claim to be "whole grain." Whole-grain bread and pasta are healthier choices than white versions, but they are not truly whole grains.

Whole grains have not been processed or cut into. Cracked grains serve their place in the diet, as they relax the body, but do not have nearly as much nutritional value as whole grains. Whole grains are complex carbohydrates and give a body energy. They are high in fiber and help stabilize blood sugar levels. They fill you up, and help with waste elimination.

Brown rice, barley, millet, quinoa, amaranth, wheat berries, and whole-oat groats are just a few of *dozens* of whole grains.

Cracked grains are *not* whole grains. Whole-wheat bread and pasta, couscous, bulgur, and polenta (cornmeal) are cracked grains. Oatmeal is probably the least processed cracked grain, as it has only been flattened or "rolled."

Both whole and cracked grains are needed in a healthy diet. Grains are amazing, and it's worth experimenting with new ones!

Amazingly-Good-For-You Brown Rice

2 cups organic short-grain (or jasmine) brown rice
4 cups water
pinch of sea salt

Rinse the rice and place in a pot with the water. Bring to a boil over high flame. Add the sea salt, then cover. Reduce heat to low, and simmer for 50 to 60 minutes. Reheat leftovers in a little water.

Serves 4–6

Rule of thumb: 2 parts water to 1 part rice

Variation: Cook 1 ½ cups of brown rice with ½ cup of either barley, millet, oats, or wheat berries.

Optional: Sprinkle with toasted pumpkin or sunflower seeds.

Creamy Brown Rice Cereal

This will definitely keep you satisfied until lunch!

1 cup cooked brown rice (can be leftover)
⅓ cup milk (can be soy, hemp, rice milk, or substitute water)
½ apple, cut into small pieces
dash of cinnamon
dash of nutmeg

Mix the rice, milk, and apple in a pan and heat on medium for 5 to 10 minutes, stirring occasionally. Top with the cinnamon and nutmeg.

Serves 1

Hato Mugi Blend

Hato mugi, or Job's tears, is actually a grass seed, but it looks like a grain because it's dried and round like a kernel of short-grained brown rice, but plumper. It's usually found in the specialty foods section with other small packages of grains like brown rice. I've also ordered it online from the Kushi Institute store.

> 2 cups brown rice, soaked overnight
> 1 cup hato mugi
> 5 to 6 cups water
> pinch of sea salt

Wash the rice and hato mugi and place in a large pot. Add the water and sea salt and bring to a boil. Cover, turn to low, and simmer for 1 hour.

Serves 4–6

Note: For a smaller amount, use ⅔ cup of brown rice and ⅓ cup of hato mugi with 2 cups of water. Of course, you can always cook hato mugi on its own as well.

Big-Treat Waffles

These waffles are a BIG treat. They're the kind of thing I have on Christmas or New Year's Day or another special occasion.

You can put the dry ingredients together the night before and leave them in a covered bowl to make the morning prep that much quicker. This recipe makes about four good-size waffles. I eat them plain straight from the waffle iron. My husband Tom likes his with organic Maine maple syrup and so do my kids. These waffles are also delicious with ¼ cup of chopped pecans or almonds mixed into the batter!

1 ½ cups cooked brown rice (see Amazingly-Good-For-You Brown Rice, p. 19)

3 tablespoons safflower oil

¼ cup rice syrup

1 cup organic soy milk (rice or hemp milk may also be used)

1 ½ cups whole wheat pastry or brown rice flour

2 teaspoons baking powder

¾ teaspoon cinnamon

¼ teaspoon nutmeg

1 tablespoon egg replacer (I use Ener-G brand) mixed with 4 tablespoons of water, or 1 egg

Combine the cooked brown rice, safflower oil, rice syrup, and soy milk in a medium saucepan. Heat on low just until the mixture is warm.

In a large mixing bowl, combine the brown rice flour, baking powder, cinnamon, and nutmeg. Set aside.

Next, beat the egg replacer with water in a mixer until stiff. Fold the egg replacer into the flour mixture, then stir in the oil, syrup, and soy milk mixture.

Preheat waffle iron. Spray with olive oil cooking spray (if you don't, they will stick). My waffle iron takes 2 to 3 minutes to cook these waffles. Enjoy!

Makes four 6- or 7-inch waffles

Aisha's Oatmeal

I met the wonderful Aisha Memon in 2002 at the Kushi Institute in Becket, Massachusetts. She came to Maine from California to take care of my children (and turn them into big fans of oatmeal!) so that I could study more at the KI.

2 cups water
2 cups apple juice
pinch of sea salt
2 1/2 to 3 cups rolled oats
1 McIntosh apple, cut into cubes

Put the water and apple juice in a pot and heat on high. Add the sea salt, rolled oats, and apple. Bring to a boil, then turn heat to low and simmer uncovered for 8 to 10 minutes. You may add more water anytime during cooking if needed for desired consistency.

Turn off heat, cover, and let sit for 5 more minutes. This allows the oatmeal to absorb all the liquid and to make a nice texture. Top with fresh (or dried) fruit, such as delicious Maine blueberries, peaches, or raisins, and toasted sunflower seeds or nuts, if desired.

Serves 4

Soothing Just-Right Porridge

If you're not feeling your best, this is an excellent way to get a little nourishment when you're not in the greatest condition to eat. It's simple:

1 cup cooked (can be leftover) brown rice (see Amazingly–Good–For–You Brown
    Rice, p. 19)
$^{1}/_{2}$ cup water

Put the cooked rice in a small pan with $^{1}/_{2}$ cup of water and bring to a boil on high. Cover, turn heat to low, and simmer for 10 to 20 minutes, adding more water if needed for the desired consistency.

Serves 1

Note: This isn't just a remedy for an upset stomach. When you're feeling chipper, you might top this healthy porridge with fresh blueberries or toasted sunflower seeds or nuts.

Corn Polenta

3 cups water
1 cup coarse ground cornmeal
$1/8$ teaspoon sea salt

Place water in a pot and bring to a boil on high. When water boils, slowly add the cornmeal, stirring quickly to dissolve any lumps.

Reduce heat to low and simmer. The cornmeal will start to thicken in a few minutes. Add the salt and simmer 5 to 10 minutes, stirring occasionally. If you want it a little creamier, add a little more water and stir as needed.

Serve immediately as a breakfast porridge or pour into a small baking dish and let it stand 15 to 30 minutes until it sets. Cut into squares and serve, or save for later and reheat by putting a small amount of oil in a cast-iron skillet and lightly frying.

Serves 3–4

Brown Rice and Lentils

1 cup green lentils
1 $1/4$ cups brown rice
1-inch piece of kombu
1 medium onion, sliced
4 cups water
$1/2$ teaspoon salt

Wash and drain the lentils and brown rice. Lay the strip of kombu in the bottom of a pan. If you're using an onion, it can be sautéed in a little olive (or sesame) oil, or added to the pot with the kombu. Then add the lentils, rice, and water. Bring to a boil on high, cover, reduce heat to low and simmer for 45 minutes. Add salt and cook for 10 more minutes.

Serves 4–6

Tom's Irish Fried Rice

A longtime runner and now a cyclist, my husband Tom Wolff has always gravitated toward healthy pursuits. So, when I started eating and cooking healthier foods it wasn't much of a stretch for him to change his diet, too. As the second oldest of nine kids, he's always known how to cook. The story goes that his parents went away on vacation one time and left the kids with a babysitter who was a terrible cook. Tom took over and became the chef, cooking for all ten of them! His repertoire now includes many healthy and appealing dishes, including delicious fried rice. His Irish Fried Rice is always a hit.

2 teaspoons olive oil
1 carrot, diced
1 medium red onion, diced
2 stalks of celery, diced
sea salt
optional: 1/4 cup sprouted adzuki beans
3 to 4 cups cooked organic brown rice (see Amazingly-Good-For-You Brown Rice, p. 19)
1 tablespoon soy sauce
2 tablespoons water
1/8 cup chopped parsley or sliced green onions

In a skillet over medium to high heat, add olive oil, carrot, onion, and celery. Sprinkle with sea salt and sauté 2 to 3 minutes. Add the beans(if desired), then spoon cooked rice evenly over the vegetable and bean mixture until it is covered. Do not stir. Sprinkle with the soy sauce and water.

Cover, turn heat to low and cook for 10 minutes. When done, gently stir vegetables into the rice. Top with parsley or green onions.

Serves 4–6

Variation: Half a pound tofu cut into small squares can be used in place of the sprouted adzuki beans. Tom usually uses tofu (added at the same time as beans), but when he tried the sprouted beans, it was a delicious experiment!

Brown Rice with Barley

2 cups organic brown rice (washed and soaked overnight in water)
1 cup whole barley (washed and soaked overnight in water)
4 ½ cups water
pinch of sea salt or piece of kombu (soaked and diced)

Put the brown rice, barley, and water in a pressure cooker over low heat and bring to a boil.

Add salt or kombu, cover, turn heat to high, and bring to pressure. Reduce heat to medium-low, place the pressure cooker on a flame deflector and cook 45 to 50 minutes. Remove from heat, allow the pressure to come down naturally, and serve.

Serves 6–8

Note: If you want to pot-boil the rice and barley instead of using a pressure cooker, use 6 cups of water. Put the rice, barley, and water into a pot. Bring to a boil on high, add salt or kombu, cover, reduce heat to low, and simmer for 1 hour and 15 minutes.

Hearty Steel-Cut Oats

All oats start from the same grains. It's just a matter of how they're cut. Rolled oats are whole oats that are rolled flat. Quick oats are rolled oats that are ground up to make them cook faster. And steel-cut oats are heartier and chewier because they are not chopped as finely.

3 cups water
1 cup steel-cut oatmeal
1 apple, cut into small pieces
pinch of sea salt
dash of cinnamon
optional: Nuts, seeds, or dried fruit

Bring water to a boil on high. Slowly stir in the ingredients. Return to boil, then turn heat to low. Simmer 30 to 40 minutes. Top with nuts, seeds, or fruit, if desired.

Serves 2–3

Pasta with Peas, Olives, and Tofu

12 ounces brown rice pasta

1 tablespoon olive oil

1 onion, chopped

1/8 teaspoon sea salt

6 ounces pitted Kalamata olives

8 ounces tofu (or other protein), cut into small cubes

1 cup peas (or other vegetable)

In a large soup pan, bring a half-pan of water to a boil, add pasta, and cook per directions. Drain and set aside.

Heat olive oil on medium heat in a cast-iron skillet, add chopped onion and sea salt. Sauté for 2 minutes, cover, and simmer for 5 more minutes. Stir onions, then add the olives and tofu. Cover and simmer for 5 to 10 more minutes (still on medium). Check the heat regularly to keep from burning and, if necessary, turn heat to low.

Add fresh peas (or other vegetable), cook on low for 5 more minutes. Add cooked pasta to the skillet. Toss for a few minutes over a low flame.

Serves 4

Loaded Vegan Lasagna

I first met Mark Boucher through my husband Tom. A few years back, my sister Ruth and I went to Mark's house in Waterville, Maine, to see his amazing garden. Mark loves growing vegetables and flowers, and Ruth and I had fun looking around his little backyard paradise. When Mark came to a potluck supper at my house, he brought this carefully crafted, fabulous vegan lasagna. Loaded with good things like carrots, this dish is absolutely luscious.

Tofu 'Ricotta'

> 2 pounds organic extra firm tofu, drained
> ¹/₂ cup water
> 1 tablespoon umeboshi plum vinegar (brown rice or other vinegar can be substituted)
> ¹/₂ cup scallions, chopped
> 1 teaspoon shoyu (soy sauce)

Place all ingredients in a large bowl, mash, and then whisk to a creamy consistency (or use a blender or food processor in batches—a bit easier). Set aside.

Sauce

> 2 to 3 pounds carrots, chopped
> 1 large onion, chopped
> 4 cloves garlic, minced
> 2 tablespoons thyme, chopped
> 1 tablespoon shoyu
> ¹/₂ cup water

Place all ingredients in a large pot, cover, and slow-cook for 2 to 3 hours, until the carrots are very tender. Mash into a sauce-like consistency (like applesauce).

Other Ingredients

> 1 box whole wheat lasagna noodles, cooked according to package directions
> 2 pounds fresh shiitake mushrooms, sliced and lightly sautéed with a bit of shoyu
> 2 pounds bok choy, sautéed with a bit of sesame oil and water
> 3 ears fresh corn (slice corn raw from the cobs)

Spread a thin layer of sauce on the bottom of a lasagna pan, place a layer of cooked lasagna noodles in the pan, then a generous layer of tofu ricotta, then mushrooms, bok choy, and fresh corn. Then spread another layer of sauce and repeat for 3 layers (the bottom and top layers should always be sauce).

Dollop spoonfuls of tofu ricotta on top. Bake at 350 degrees for 45 minutes, loosely covered. Remove cover and bake another 20 minutes until the dollops of tofu are browned. Let cool and garnish with 2 thinly chopped scallions.

Serves 12

Mark says: "*I based the ricotta recipe from one I got off the Internet, and I dreamed up the rest of this!*"

Amaranth and Apricots

Amaranth, a grain eaten by the Incas, is high in the amino acid lysine, containing twice as much as other grains like wheat and rice. It's also higher in minerals like calcium, iron, and magnesium than other grains. Quite a powerhouse contained in each of those tiny grains, and they cook up into a nice porridge!

Serve this for breakfast, with sides of steamed kale and carrots. Amaranth is extremely good for you.

> 1 1/2 **cups water**
> 1/2 **cup amaranth**
> **pinch of sea salt**
> 1 to 2 **apricots, chopped**

Combine water, amaranth, and salt in a small saucepan. Bring to a boil, then reduce heat to a simmer. Cover and cook over low heat for 15 minutes, or until the water is absorbed. Stir in apricots.

Serves 2

Mile-a-Millet!

Millet is a grain equal to brown rice in nutrients. Talk about super-foods—high fiber is one of millet's great health benefits.

   1 cup millet
   1 cup butternut squash or other vegetable (remove seeds and cut into 1-inch cubes)
   3 cups water (more if you'd like it creamier)
   pinch of sea salt

Place millet, squash, and/or other vegetables, and water in a pot. Bring to a boil over medium heat, add sea salt, and cover.

Turn heat to low and simmer for 35 minutes. Remove millet from heat and serve warm.

Serves 3–4

Note: Corn, onions, carrots, parsnips, and rutabagas also work well in this dish, or millet may be cooked and eaten plain.

Sprinkle with toasted sunflower seeds and serve with a side of streamed greens, for a hearty breakfast (Or lunch or dinner!).

Summery Quinoa Salad

Quinoa is a protein-rich grain native to South America and it's really a seed, cooked like a whole grain. It only takes 15 minutes to cook, unlike brown rice, barley, or other whole grains, which take about an hour. So it's a quick and easy favorite of mine.

2 cups cooked quinoa

1 red pepper (and/or carrot), diced

black olives, diced

1 zucchini, diced

1 cup cooked (or canned) garbanzo beans

1 cup peas

¹/₄ cup sunflower seeds

¹/₄ cup parsley

¹/₄ cup lemon juice

¹/₄ cup wheat-free soy sauce or ¹/₂ teaspoon sea salt

¹/₄ cup olive oil

Toss ingredients together and enjoy with steamed greens and a soup if desired.

Serves 6

Vegan Pad Thai

1 tablespoon sesame oil

1 tablespoon hot chili sesame oil

3 large cloves garlic, minced

1 onion, cut in half, sliced thinly into half moons

1 large carrot, shredded

1 (16-ounce) package organic tofu, cut into 1/2-inch squares

1 (14-ounce) package Pad Thai white rice noodles (or a 16-ounce package of Tinkyada
    brand brown rice pasta noodles), cooked according to package directions

3 scallions, sliced thinly on a diagonal

1/2 cup fresh cilantro, chopped

1 1/2 cups fresh mung bean sprouts

1/4 cup peanuts, chopped

Sauce

1/2 cup water

1/2 cup brown rice syrup

2 tablespoons Tamari wheat-free soy sauce

optional: 3/4 tablespoon paprika

optional: 3/4 teaspoon chili peppers

Mix the water, rice, syrup, and soy sauce (and optional ingredients, if using) and set the sauce aside.

Blend the oils in a large skillet (or wok), heat on high, and sauté the garlic for 1 minute. Add onion, reduce heat to medium, and sauté for another minute or two.

Add the carrot and tofu and cook for another 5 minutes. Add the sauce (set aside) and simmer for 3 to 5 minutes.

Add the cooked noodles and stir so that sauce thoroughly coats them. Mix in scallions, cilantro and bean sprouts. Garnish with chopped peanuts. Serve immediately.

Serves 6–8

John's Powerhouse Pasta

Dr. John Herzog, an osteopathic surgeon in Falmouth, Maine, contacted me a couple of years ago while making connections with others interested in a plant-based way of eating. He had tried to lower his high cholesterol through medication, but didn't like the side effects. So he decided to adopt a plant-based diet. His cholesterol levels quickly improved and dropped eventually to 150 mg/dl. The dramatic decrease prompted him to take on a research study, and he's now a strong advocate of healthier eating. John brought this dish to a potluck supper at my home and it was a big hit!

Pesto

- 1 tablespoon olive oil
- 3 cloves garlic
- 2 cups fresh basil, chopped
- 1/4 cup pine nuts (can be roasted 2 to 3 minutes in a cast-iron skillet)
- 1/2 cup pitted Kalamata olives, sliced
- *optional:* sea salt or pepper to taste

John says: "I use a Braun immersion blender and blend the oil and garlic first, then add the basil. Add nuts and Kalamata olives at the end, unblended."

Cook 12 ounces of pasta according to package directions and drain. Toss pasta and pesto and serve.

Serves 6–8

Elegant Tofu Polenta

My sister-in-law Sheryl Wolff made this polenta recipe when I visited her in Pennsylvania. It was delicious hot out of the oven at Sheryl's house, and just as good at room temperature on my train ride home to Boston the next day.

  5 cups water
  1 bouillon cube (vegan if preferred)
  1 teaspoon sea salt (Sheryl used a beautiful pink "sea salt" from Utah)
  2 cups cornmeal
  $1/2$ cups roasted pecans
  2 pounds firm tofu (Soyboy Organic is a great brand)
  1 tablespoon soy sauce
  1 teaspoon mirin (this is a Japanese cooking wine)
  1 teaspoon sesame oil
  1 teaspoon olive oil
  optional: 1 tablespoon lemon juice
  1 clove garlic, minced
  sprig of rosemary for garnish

Preheat oven to 350 degrees.

In a medium pot, bring the water, bouillon, and sea salt to a boil. Add cornmeal and stir until the mixture thickens. Turn heat to low, cover, and simmer for 20 minutes, stirring occasionally. Pour the mixture into an 8- x 4-inch baking dish. Leave to set for 1 hour or longer.

Puree pecans with remaining ingredients, include 1/4 cup of water if necessary.

Pour tofu mixture over polenta, and bake for 30 minutes at 350 degrees. Cut into squares and serve, with a mint leaf or two on each square for beauty if desired.

Serves 6–8

Brown Rice with Black Soybeans (or Black Beans)

For this dish, I used to try to find Hokkaido (Japan) Organic Black Soybeans, as they're high quality and known for the mineral-rich soil in which they're grown. I've recently started using Maine-grown black beans and these work well with rice. (The local beans have a softness and are much more flavorful, making them a cut above all others!) Pair this with some farmers' market broccoli and kale to make a light summer meal!

1 1/3 cup dried organic black soybeans or black beans
1 cup organic long grain brown rice
3 cups water
pinch of salt

Soak the beans in water overnight. Drain and place the beans in a pot, then add the rice and water and bring to a boil on high. Reduce heat to low, cover, and simmer for one hour. Add the salt and continue cooking for 5 to 10 more minutes.

Serves 6

Family Reactions to Change

People often ask how I dealt with my family's reactions when I started eating a plant-based diet to help me heal from breast cancer.

The first situation that comes to mind is my dad's questioning the diet because I was losing weight. Makes sense that he would be concerned. I know my dad loves me, and he had just seen my mom lose a lot of weight before passing away from colon cancer. My father has a lot of common sense and he listens. Not everyone does. So I explained about the food being whole grains, beans, and vegetables—*real* unprocessed foods, high in nutrients, high in fiber, low in fat. I told him I was starting to feel better than I had in years.

As time went on, my dad saw that I *was* eating, I wasn't nauseous, and in fact I was starting to show signs of good health. I was sleeping through the night, my ulcerative colitis and other digestive problems had gone away completely, my skin cleared and glowed, my moods were more stable, and anxiety attacks went away completely. I was getting healthy! He saw that I was eating good-quality and generous portions of food (I ate a *lot*!) and his fears were diminished.

My body and mind were beginning to heal and I was sure this was my path. Eating this way made me feel good. Because of this, I projected a certain strength and confidence. When we're confident about what we're doing, other people eventually relax and respect our choices (even though *they* may not want to adopt the same way of eating). That's how it was with my dad and me.

I know some people have quite a hard time with their families when they make big changes. I've experienced other people's fear, negativity, or just plain inconvenience (to them) about my eating in a healthy way. So I understand. Making a few healthy changes in your diet also can remind people of what *they* could/should be doing.

beans & bean products

Digesting Beans

For people starting out eating beans, one of the most common complaints is that beans cause gas or stomach aches. This can be avoided by starting with small amounts ($1/8$ to $1/4$ cup) and by chewing well.

Lots of experts recommend chewing each mouthful 100 times, especially for people with digestive problems or constipation. Other counselors suggest 50 times per mouthful.

Many people have a hard time with this concept, so I suggest chewing 15 times and working up to 50.

Soaking beans the night before you cook them, throwing away the soaking water in the morning, refilling with new water, and also adding a postage-stamp-size piece of kombu will all help make the beans more digestible.

Starting with bean soups may be easier on the digestive system. Try pureeing half (or all) of the beans and adding them back to the soup as a base.

One of the most commonly asked questions I get is: What size portion of beans do you eat? I usually eat $1/3$ to $1/2$ cup per meal.

SIMPLY SOAK

It's easy to get in the habit of taking out a bag (or jar) of beans, emptying (or measuring out a cup or more, if that's your style) some into a saucepan, covering them with water, and leaving them to soak overnight. This takes all of 2 or 3 minutes. The next day, drain off the water, add new water to cover the beans by about an inch, and cook them.

This is not difficult! If you forget to soak beans overnight, soaking them 4 to 5 hours the same day works just fine, too.

Gingerly Chickpeas

Chickpeas are bursting with nutrients. They're a great source of plant protein and calcium, and they're delicious!

2 cups chickpeas, soaked overnight
1 onion, peeled
$1/4$ teaspoon sea salt
$1/2$ cup fresh parsley, chopped
2 tablespoons fresh ginger juice (grated ginger squeezed to make juice)

Drain the soaking water for chickpeas. Place them in a pot and add water to cover an inch or more.

Place the onion in the middle of the chickpeas. Bring to a boil, cover, and reduce heat to low. Simmer for 1 hour. Add salt, stir, and simmer for 10 more minutes.

When done, pour off a cup or so of the cooking water and set aside. This can be used to thin the chickpea mixture if it's too thick. Use a potato masher to mash the chickpeas and onion until halfway pureed. Grate some ginger and squeeze the juice into the mixture to taste. Garnish with parsley. Serve on their own or with brown rice.

Serves 6–8

Lentil Loaf

2 cups dried red lentils
1-inch piece of dried wakame (reconstituted in water 3 to 5 minutes)
1 onion, diced
$^1/_2$ teaspoon sea salt
3 ribs celery, diced
2 carrots, diced
2 shiitake mushrooms, diced
optional: 1 teaspoon Italian seasoning
1 teaspoon tamari or shoyu sauce
1 teaspoon ume (plum) vinegar
$^1/_3$ cup pan-roasted almonds or pecans, chopped
1 $^1/_4$ cups rolled oats

Preheat oven to 350 degrees.

Put lentils in a pot with enough water to cover. Wash them by rubbing them between your palms to release the outer skin. Drain the water and refill the pot with 4 cups of clean water. Add wakame. Bring to a boil, reduce heat to low, cover, and cook for 40 minutes.

While the lentils are cooking, sauté the onion in olive oil on medium-high heat. Add sea salt and cook for 1 to 2 minutes more. Add celery, carrot, shiitake, and optional seasoning, sauté for 3 to 5 minutes more. Stir in shoyu sauce and ume vinegar and simmer for 3 to 5 minutes.

In a cast-iron skillet, toast almonds or pecans on medium-high heat for 5 minutes or until slightly browned, stirring occasionally. Chop into small pieces.

Combine the lentils, cooked vegetables, and $^1/_3$ of the oats. Add a tablespoon of olive oil if desired. Stir to mix. Add $^1/_4$ cup more water if needed. Coat a 9- x 12-inch pan with olive oil and spread the lentil mixture in the pan. Sprinkle with the remaining rolled oats and the almonds or pecans.

Bake for 25 to 30 minutes.

Serves 8–10

Tempeh Lemon Bake

    2 (8-ounce) packages tempeh
    1 large onion, sliced
    juice of two lemons (or other citrus combo)
    $1/4$ cup olive oil
    3 tablespoons soy sauce
    optional: 2 garlic cloves, minced

Preheat oven to 400 degrees.

Combine all ingredients. Marinate for 3 hours. Bake in a 9- x 13-inch pan for 30 minutes, basting occasionally.

Note: Before marinating the tempeh, I cube it and put it in a saucepan with 1-2 cups of water. Bring water to a boil on high flame, reduce heat to low, and simmer for 10 minutes. This makes the tempeh softer and easier to marinate.

Serves 6–8

Backyard Bar-B-Q Pan-Fried Tempeh

This is great served with steamed brown rice with toasted pumpkin seeds and veggies.

    1 (8-ounce) package organic tempeh, sliced into thin strips
    Oil to cover bottom of a cast-iron skillet

Heat oil on medium-high heat and fry the tempeh strips until they are brown and crispy. Drain on a paper towel to soak up any excess oil.

Dip in grain mustard if desired.

Serves 2–3

Old Bay Tofu Cakes with Cream Horseradish and Creole Mustard Sauce over Shaved Fennel Slaw

Kathy Freston is an amazing life coach and writer, Oprah's go-to pal, and a wonderful, gentle, helpful woman. I had already become a fan through her best-selling books, Quantum Wellness and The One, when I met her for the first time a couple of years ago at a Physicians Committee for Responsible Medicine fundraiser she hosted in New York City. I immediately liked her. She's gorgeous and famous, but so down to earth. Sounds a little funny, but she reminds me of Glinda the Good Witch from The Wizard of Oz because of her warmth, vulnerability, and kindness. We are both trying to nudge people gently toward good health—I like what she says about leaning into a healthy lifestyle and concur about how small steps toward that make a difference. This recipe comes from her favorite chef, Tal Ronnen. It's delish. Make this for a special occasion!

Fennel Slaw

1 $1/2$ pounds fresh fennel slaw, shaved very thinly

1 cup julienne-cut carrots

1 tablespoon fresh dill, chopped

2 tablespoons fresh lemon juice

1 tablespoon extra-virgin olive oil

$1/2$ teaspoon freshly grated lemon zest

$1/2$ teaspoon salt

Mix all ingredients together in a large bowl. Set aside.

Sauce

$3/4$ cup mayonnaise (try veggie mayonnaise or mustard)

$3/4$ cup sour cream (try Follow Your Heart brand)

2 $1/2$ tablespoons bottled horseradish

2 tablespoons coarsely ground Creole mustard

juice of 1 lemon (about 1 $1/2$ tablespoons)

1 teaspoon sea salt

freshly cracked pepper to taste

Combine all the ingredients except the pepper in a bowl and mix well. Adjust seasoning with black pepper. Refrigerate until ready to serve.

Cakes

    $1/2$ cup finely diced onion
    $1/2$ cup freshly diced carrot
    2 tablespoons vegetable oil
    2 teaspoons minced garlic
    2 pounds firm tofu
    $1/4$ cup nutritional yeast
    2 $1/2$ tablespoons cornstarch
    1 teaspoon salt
    $1/2$ teaspoon ground white pepper
    juice of 1 lime

Sauté the onion and carrot in oil until soft, about 3 to 5 minutes. Add garlic and sauté 1 minute longer. Let cool completely.

Add the remaining ingredients, mix well. Let cool in the refrigerator for 30 minutes.

To Assemble:

    2 cups brown rice flour
    3 tablespoons Old Bay seasoning
    1 teaspoon salt
    1 $1/2$ cups unsweetened soy milk
    2 cups canola oil

Mix rice flour, Old Bay, and salt together. Form the tofu cake mixture by hand. Immerse each cake in the soy milk. Dredge cakes in seasoned flour, coating each well.

Refrigerate the cakes for 30 minutes to set firm.

Sauté at medium-high in canola oil (make certain that oil is about halfway up the side of each cake) until browned on both sides and heated completely through.

Serve the cakes over a small amount of slaw and top with sauce.

Makes 12–14 small (approximately 2-ounce) cakes

Optional: Place $2/3$ cup of baby greens on the plate, then the slaw on top.

Beloved Burritos

1 cup black beans
1 cup pinto beans
$^1/_2$ teaspoon of sea salt
1 package (8–10) large whole wheat or corn tortillas (organic if possible)
4 cups cooked organic brown rice (2 cups uncooked; See Amazingly-Good-For-You
    Brown Rice, p. 19)
optional: 2 chopped avocados, salsa
Half a head of lettuce or Napa cabbage, thinly sliced
5 cucumber sour pickles, chopped (I love Bubbie's brand)
optional: salsa

Tofu Sour Cream

1 (14-ounce) package extra-firm tofu
$^1/_2$ cup fresh cilantro (or parsley), washed and chopped
1 tablespoon freshly squeezed lemon or lime juice

Beans: Rinse the pinto beans and black beans and soak overnight. Drain the beans. (You can also use canned beans.) Refill the pan with water to cover by one inch. Bring to a boil on high. Reduce heat to low, cover, and simmer for 1 hour. Add salt, cover, and cook for 15 minutes more.

Tofu Sour Cream: Boil the tofu in 2 inches of water for 5 minutes. Drain the water. Add cilantro (or parsley). Blend in a food processor with lemon or lime juice.

To steam tortillas: Add an inch of water to a large pan. Boil water to steam. Place colander or steamer basket inside the pan (not touching water!). Place tortillas, one at a time, in the colander or steam basket for about a minute or until soft. The pan should be uncovered.

To build burritos: Place a soft tortilla on a plate. Spread a spoonful of the tofu sour cream thinly on the tortilla. Spread pinto/black beans over sour cream. Spread rice next. Add avocado, if desired. Add lettuce or Napa cabbage, chopped pickles, and optional salsa. Roll and enjoy!

French Scramble

Rory Freedman, author of Skinny Bitch, *knows how to make a fab breakfast. I met Rory at Kathy Freston's book celebration and again at the Physicians Committee for Responsible Medicine gala in Los Angeles in April 2010. I had read her books,* Skinny Bitch *and* Skinny Bitch in the Kitch *(written with best friend Kim Barnouin, a holistic nutritionist). Rory doesn't suffer fools! Which reminds me of my college-age daughter Cammie, who loved* Skinny Bitch *and shared it with all of her friends! Cammie has been eating healthy since she was 8 (when I changed my diet!), and Rory reinforced for her that making healthy choices makes you healthily thin and radiantly beautiful! I love Rory's straight talk, backed up by sound science. She and Kim have followed their hearts and started an empire in the process that is helping many women (and men, Skinny Bastards) to get healthier and lose weight. Here's a favorite Rory breakfast dish.*

14 to 16 ounces firm or extra-firm tofu, crumbled (use your hands or a fork)

4 ounces vegan Jack, cheddar, or American cheese, shredded

3 scallions, sliced

2 cloves garlic, minced

2 tablespoons nutritional yeast flakes

1 tablespoon tamari or soy sauce

$1/2$ teaspoon turmeric

$1/2$ teaspoon fine sea salt

$1/2$ teaspoon pepper

$1/2$ tablespoon refined coconut oil

1 cup (sliced) mushrooms (any kind, or a combination)

1 cup sliced onions

2 cups fresh spinach leaves, chopped if desired

In a large bowl, combine the tofu, vegan cheese, scallions, garlic, yeast flakes, tamari, turmeric, salt, and pepper. Set aside. In a large, nonstick skillet over medium heat, melt the coconut oil. Add the mushrooms and onions and cook, stirring occasionally, until tender, about 1 $1/2$ minutes. Stir in the spinach, a handful at a time if necessary, and cook until wilted, about 1 minute. Stir in the tofu mixture and cook, stirring occasionally, for 3 to 4 minutes, or until any liquid has evaporated and the mixture is hot. Serve immediately.

Serves 3–4

Squashed Adzuki

2 cups adzuki beans, soaked overnight (or 4–5 hours the day of)
¼ to ½ butternut squash (keep outer skin on), cubed
1 onion, peeled
¼ teaspoon sea salt

Once you have soaked the beans, drained them, and added new water, push the whole onion into the bottom of the pot. Add the cubed squash. Bring beans to a boil on high, then cover, turn to low, and simmer for 1 hour (or more if desired).

Ten minutes before you're done cooking the beans, add the sea salt. (For each additional cup of beans, add ⅛ teaspoon of salt.)

Serves 6–8

Optional: Enjoy on a bed of whole grains!

Note: The beans can be refrigerated and reheated as needed. They also freeze well.

Tempeh Salad

A great alternative to the classic luncheon tuna salad!

3 (8-ounce) packages tempeh (I like Litelife organic garden vegetable type for this)

1 purple onion, diced

3 ribs of celery, diced

2 scallions, thinly sliced

1/2 cup fresh cilantro, chopped

optional: 1/3 cup cucumber pickle relish (I use Bubbie's brand)

1/2 cup mayonnaise (I use veggie mayonnaise, which is egg and dairy free)

2 tablespoons shoyu sauce

1 tablespoon apple cider vinegar (I like Bragg's brand)

1 teaspoon ume vinegar

Cut the tempeh into smaller pieces (I cut it into triangles), put into a pot, and add water to about halfway up. Bring to a boil, turn heat to low, cover, and simmer for 20 minutes.

Drain, cool, and crumble the tempeh into smaller pieces with your hands (it softens and crumbles more easily after cooking it). Add the onion, celery, scallions, cilantro, and cucumber relish and mix together in a large mixing bowl.

In a separate small mixing bowl, mix the mayonnaise, shoyu sauce, apple cider vinegar, and ume vinegar. Add to the tempeh and mix.

Serves 8–10

Marinated Tofu Stir Fry

1 pound tofu
$^1/_2$ cup onion, sliced
1 cup cabbage, shredded
1 cup carrots, sliced
1 cup broccoli, chopped
optional: add collards, mushrooms, or corn, as desired
4 to 6 cups cooked brown rice (noodles can be substituted)

Marinade

2 tablespoons mirin (a Japanese rice wine found in health food stores)
4 tablespoons soy sauce
$^1/_4$ to$^1/_2$ cup water
pinch of sea salt
2 tablespoons rice syrup
$^1/_4$ cup fresh cilantro, chopped
2 tablespoons sesame oil
2 tablespoons toasted sesame seeds
2 tablespoons fresh ginger juice (grate ginger, squeeze out juice, discard pulp)
2 tablespoons ume or brown rice vinegar
2 green onions, thinly sliced
optional: pepper

Combine all the marinade ingredients and marinate the tofu for at least 2 hours.

In a cast-iron skillet over high heat, bring tofu and marinade to a boil. Turn heat to low and sauté for 2 to 3 minutes; cover and steam for 5 more minutes. You may add a little more water if marinade cooks down. Remove from skillet; put in a covered dish and set aside.

Sauté the vegetables in sesame oil on medium-high heat. Add the salt and a little of the marinade. Reduce heat to low, cover, and simmer for 3 to 5 minutes.

To serve, layer rice (or noodles), then veggies, and tofu on top, squeeze a small amount of ginger juice to taste. Garnish with green onions.

Serves 4–6

Garlic Spaghetti

This is a favorite recipe of my sister Liz and my brother-in-law Steve Bennett—people I've cooked with since "going healthy." We've inspired each other, and the story of their son Stephen's amazing recovery from reflux is on my web site.

1 tablespoon olive or other oil

6 cloves garlic, sliced thinly

1 (8-ounce) package of organic tofu, drained and cubed

$1/8$ teaspoon sea salt or 1 tablespoon soy sauce

1 (12-ounce) package of whole wheat or rice pasta, cooked

juice from 2-inch piece of ginger (grate, squeeze out juice, discard pulp)

2 green onions, sliced thinly, diagonally

Heat oil on medium in a cast-iron skillet. Add the garlic. Keep heat low enough to keep from burning, and cook until the garlic is soft and slightly brown, about 3 to 5 minutes.

Add tofu and cook 10 to 15 minutes. Add salt or soy sauce and a little more oil (or water) if desired. Slightly mash some of the tofu while cooking.

Add cooked spaghetti noodles to the skillet and cook for another 5 minutes. Turn off heat. Add ginger juice to noodles. Garnish with green onions.

Serves 4–6

Stovetop Beans

Growing up in Maine, I remember eating beans almost weekly on Saturday nights or at family get-togethers at Sebago Lake. (We usually had beans and hotdogs.) This is my healthier version minus the dogs. Instead of salt pork, which my mom used for flavor, I use Fakin Bacon (a bean product) for a meaty, smoky flavor (there are so many good substitutes for unhealthy flavorings in beans). Instead of molasses, for a little sweetness, I used apple butter. The really great thing about the beans I use is that they're grown locally in Maine and pesticide free (dried white pea or navy beans). I often buy them at Lois' Natural Marketplace in Scarborough, Maine.

2 cups navy beans, rinsed and soaked overnight in water
1 (whole) onion, peeled,
optional: 1 (8-ounce) package tempeh, chopped
1/4 to 1/2 teaspoon sea salt
1 tablespoon grain mustard
1 cup apple butter (I use Pastor Chuck's brand)

Drain soaked beans, add new water to cover. Bring to a boil, cook on high, then reduce heat to low and cook for 1 hour. Check water while cooking to make sure the beans stay covered, adding more water if needed. Add the onion to the bottom of the pot. It will cook down and come apart, flavoring the beans, so no need to chop it. Add tempeh now, if using.

After an hour, check the beans for doneness. Take one bean on a spoon and blow on it. If the skin comes off easily, it's done. Salt should be added at this time. If the beans are not done, cook for 15 more minutes and check again. These small beans usually cook quickly, within an hour or so. Add mustard and apple butter and stir.

Serves 10–12

Good Egg Café Tempeh Hash

Mary Ledue Paine co-owns The Pepperclub/Good Egg Café in Portland, Maine. The Good Egg is THE place for breakfast in Portland. This is one of my favorite treats there: Tempeh Hash. Mary comes from a big Irish family and grew up in the Munjoy Hill section of Portland, so she still likes to be in the neighborhood. This is both my favorite breakfast and dinner place. Mary and her staff know how to cook! They have the best breakfasts, with many vegan and vegetarian options, including blueberry pancakes, tofu scrambles, red potatoes and vegan hash. If you come to Portland, you have to eat there!

> 8 ounces organic plain tempeh, crumbled
> 2 tablespoons Bragg's Liquid Aminos (or wheat-free soy)
> 1 tablespoon black pepper

Preheat oven to 400 degrees.

Mix the liquid aminos or soy with the pepper to make the marinade. Marinate tempeh, then bake for 20 minutes.

Combine with:

> 1 cup minced onion
> 1 cup grated carrot
> $1/2$ cup chopped flat parsley
> 1 $1/2$ medium baked potatoes, chilled and coarsely chopped
> 2 tablespoons onion powder
> kosher salt and black pepper to taste

Toss all ingredients together. Fry up the hash in a cast-iron pan with a little canola or olive oil until bowned and heated through. Serve hot with your favorite vegetables and homemade toast, and a little hot sauce, if desired.

Serves 2–4, depending on appetites

Optional: While hash is browning, add fresh chopped broccoli and large leafy spinach or rainbow chard.

Corn Pona Lisa (Black Bean and Corn Bread Casserole)

My friend Lisa Silverman was my first healthy-foods cooking instructor. Her macrobiotic cooking classes in her home in Portland, Maine, were a lifeline back to good health when I started improving my diet to help heal from breast cancer. At the time, Lisa was making macrobiotic "take-out" meals three days a week, and I was a grateful recipient. I continued to take her classes for a few years and then she encouraged me to teach cooking classes to others, which had never crossed my mind until that day. I filled in for her at The Cancer Community Center in South Portland and continued to teach there once a month for the next three years. She recently revitalized her Five Seasons Cooking School and is preparing wonderful meals again. Lisa is one of the most relaxed people I know—she inspires me and has taught me to be more relaxed, too.

2 cups dried black turtle beans (soaked overnight with a 2-inch piece kombu)
2 tablespoons olive oil
1 large onion, diced
1 clove garlic, minced
$1/2$ teaspoon sea salt
kernels from 4 ears corn (uncooked)
1 teaspoon ground cumin
1 tablespoon ginger juice
2 tablespoons shoyu
$1/4$ cup chopped fresh cilantro
2 teaspoons corn or olive oil, for pan

Cornbread Topping

2 $1/2$ cups cornmeal
1 $1/2$ cups whole wheat pastry flour
1 $1/3$ cups unbleached white flour
3 tablespoons baking powder
1 teaspoon sea salt
1 $1/4$ cups water
1 $1/3$ cups soy milk
$2/3$ cup light olive oil
$1/2$ cup maple syrup
$1/2$ teaspoon vanilla extract

Preheat oven to 400 degrees.

After beans and kombu have soaked, discard soaking water.

Slice the kombu into thin strips. Place the beans and kombu in a 4- or 5-liter pressure cooker and add water until it covers the beans by 1 inch. Close the pressure cooker and bring to pressure. Place a flame deflector under the pressure cooker, reduce heat to medium-low, and cook for 30 minutes (if you don't have a pressure cooker, cook the beans in a saucepan with kombu over medium-low heat for 1 1/2 hours).

While beans are cooking, heat olive oil in a skillet over medium heat. Sauté the onions, garlic, sea salt, and corn until the onions are translucent, about 5 minutes. Grate a 2-inch piece of ginger into a pulp, then squeeze out 1 tablespoon of juice.

Add cumin, ginger juice, and shoyu to the onions and cook for another 5 minutes. When the beans are cooked, add them to the onion mixture. Mix in the cilantro. Pour the mixture into a lightly oiled 9- by 13-inch casserole dish—use corn or olive oil.

Sift together the dry cornbread topping ingredients and then in a separate bowl blend together the wet ingredients. Mix them together until they are just blended. Pour the batter over the black-bean mixture and bake for 40 to 45 minutes. Let cool at least 15 minutes before serving.

Serves 12

Jacob's Creamy Cattle Beans

Local beans tend to need less soaking and less cooking time.

> 2 cups Jacob's Cattle Beans (I use Maine grown, pesticide-free)
> 2 onions
> 4 Gala apples, skin-on, cut and diced (I like organic from Ricker Hill Orchards
> in Turner, Maine)
> 3/4 teaspoon sea salt

Cover dried beans with water and soak 6 hours or overnight. Drain the beans and cover with water by 1 to 2 inches. Bring to a boil over high heat. Reduce heat to low, cover, and simmer for 1 hour.

Peel the onion and quarter. Add to the beans and simmer for 30 minutes. Add diced apples and more water if needed. Bring back to a boil, cover, reduce heat to low, and simmer for 30 more minutes.

Test for softness, and cook longer as needed. Add sea salt when beans are tender and cook for 10 to 15 more minutes.

Serves 2–4

Hip Chick's Hambulghur Helper

I met the hilarious Jessica Porter when she was living in Portland, Maine, and helping my friend and cooking school owner Lisa Silverman prepare healthy meals. Jess was also practicing hypnosis and I had a few extremely helpful sessions with her. Jess gave me an early copy of her book, The Hip Chick's Guide to Macrobiotics, *and I took it with me on vacation. I laughed until I cried, and wished that I had written this book! Since then, I've become a huge Jess fan. She's also an actress and comedienne (The Zen Comic). I believe I'll one day be watching her on her own weekly TV show.*

2 tablespoons toasted sesame oil

8 ounces tempeh, sliced into bite-size cubes

1 medium onion, diced

$^1/_8$ teaspoon sea salt

1 large carrot, cut into matchsticks

2 cups bulgur wheat

1 cup whole wheat rotini or elbow noodles

5 cups water

3 tablespoons shoyu

2 tablespoons mirin

$^1/_8$ teaspoon brown rice vinegar

kernels from 1 ear of corn

2 stalks celery, diced

In a large frying pan, heat 1 tablespoon of sesame oil over medium heat. When hot (but not smoking), add tempeh, frying the cubes until brown and crispy. Remove from heat and let drain on a paper towel. Set aside.

In a large saucepan, heat 1 tablespoon of sesame oil over medium heat. Add the onion and salt and sauté until translucent. Add the carrot and sauté a few minutes. Pour in the bulghur wheat and noodles, stirring them into the vegetables. Fold in tempeh. Seperately, mix the water, shoyu, mirin, and vinegar together, then add to the tempeh and pasta mixture.

Bring to a boil uncovered, reduce heat to low, cover, and place on flame deflector. Let simmer for 15 minutes. Add the corn and celery. Cook for 5 more minutes. Remove from heat and let sit a couple of minutes to prevent sticking.

Serves 8

Sweet & Sour Pinto Beans

    1 cup pinto beans, soaked overnight in water to cover
    3 cups water
    1-inch piece of kombu
    1 large onion, peeled
    1 carrot, diced
    shoyu or tamari soy sauce
    1 tablespoon barley malt
    1 teaspoon umeboshi or rice vinegar
    1 to 2 teaspoons stone-ground mustard

Drain the beans, add water (3 cups or more) to cover by 1 inch. Add the kombu and the whole onion. Bring to boil on high heat, turn to low, and simmer for 1 hour.

Add the carrot, soy sauce, and barley malt. Cook for 10 minutes. Stir in the vinegar and mustard.

Serve with a whole grain (such as brown rice, millet, barley, or quinoa) and vegetable(s) of choice. Make sure to chew each mouthful well. This is the key to digestibility!

Serves 2–4

The Dirty Dozen and The Cleanest 12

I keep this list posted on my refrigerator. It's from the Environmental Working Group's 'Shopper's Guide to Pesticides in Produce. The first list includes the fruits and vegetables on which growers use the highest concentrations of pesticides. The second list is of those crops that receive the lowest amount of pesticides.

buy these organic	lowest in pesticides
Peaches	Onions
Apples	Avocado
Sweet Bell Peppers	Sweet Corn (frozen)
Celery	Pineapples
Nectarines	Asparagus
Strawberries	Sweet Peas (frozen)
Cherries	Kiwi Fruit
Pears	Bananas
Grapes (imported)	Cabbage
Spinach	Broccoli
Lettuces	Papaya
Potatoes	Mango

vegetables

Like Mom Said, Eat Your Vegetables!

My No. 1 piece of advice for anyone wanting to improve his/her health is to add more fresh vegetables to their diet. A great goal is 5 to 9 servings per day. If that sounds too daunting, start with 2 to 3 a day. Or even just one! Start wherever you feel comfortable.

Think you don't like vegetables? Start with small amounts. And, here's an important tip: The more you cut sugar out of your diet, the better vegetables will taste.

We need vegetables and fruits to relax our bodies. And if we don't eat enough of them, we'll crave sugar to relax it. (Life in balance!)

Many vegetables can be easily steamed, boiled, baked, pan roasted with a little olive oil, grilled, or eaten raw (but chew thoroughly!). These are just a few suggestions on my list of root, round, and leafy vegetables: broccoli, beets, burdock, carrots, celery, collards, daikon, dandelion greens, green beans, fennel bulb, kale, leeks, mushrooms, onions, parsnips, rutabaga, radish, squash (many kinds!), turnip, watercress, yam, zucchini . . . and on and on!

When preparing vegetables, remember that the recipe doesn't have to be difficult or gourmet (unless you want). Keep it simple!

When you commit to eating more veggies, you'll be surprised how much more full you feel (especially if you add a little oil). This will enable you to cut down on your animal protein portions (if you eat them). Vegetables are high in fiber and low in fat.

So, go to your grocery store, look around, and find something new in the produce section. Make a point to try new vegetables—whatever kind you're drawn to or whatever catches your attention.

EAT THE TOPS!

Did you know that you can eat the tops (stems and leaves) of carrots, too? Slice the carrots and steam them in a little water in a covered saucepan for a few minutes. Then add in the green tops, finely chopped, and a little soy sauce or umeboshi vinegar, then steam it all a few more minutes. Delicious and very good for you!

PROPER TECHNIQUE

It's good to be reminded of the proper technique to use for chopping so you don't cut your fingers as I've done from time to time.

Curl your fingers while holding the vegetables (the first knuckles after the tips of your fingers should be resting on the cutting surface) so that the flat of the knife blade rests against the side of your curled index finger, keeping it a good distance from your curled fingertips.

CUTTING RIBBONS

Looking for another hearty, leafy green, cancer-fighting vegetable? Collard greens, cousin to kale, are a great source of non-dairy calcium and are loaded with good-for-you substances. They have a mild smoky flavor. When cutting a bunch of collards, I cut out the stems, layer them one on top of the other, and roll them up (the long way), then I slice them into thin ribbons.

I usually slice the stems separately, and thinly on an angle, then steam them for about 5 minutes. You don't have to eat the stem, but it's a good way to use the "whole food." If I'm feeling fancy, I'll slice an onion thinly into half-moon pieces (cut the onion in half from top to bottom and slice thinly from side to side). I sauté the onion in a skillet with a little olive oil and a pinch of sea salt. After 2 to 3 minutes, I add the collards and a sprinkle of tamari wheat-free soy sauce, and sauté another 3 to 4 minutes. Sometimes I add a few slivered almonds or walnuts.

VEGGIES FOR BREAKFAST? DEFINITELY!

When you eat veggies, you crave veggies. Dubious? Well, try it and prove me wrong!

It's really true. I start every day with vegetables. Quite the switch from pastries and cold sugary cereals, and never in a million years (before my recovery from cancer) would I have predicted I'd be eating vegetables first thing in the morning. But now, that's me.

Whole grains and veggies have been my typical morning foods for the past twelve years. Do you eat veggies for breakfast? I highly recommend them!

Steamed Kale

Many days, I steam a little kale in the morning, let it sit, drained, in a pot and nibble on it throughout the morning.

> 1 bunch kale, rinsed and chopped into bite–size pieces (stem and all)
> $^1/_2$ cup water
> pinch of sea salt

Put water, kale, and a pinch of salt into a pot with a lid. Bring to a boil over high heat, turn to low, and simmer for 3 to 5 minutes. Drain.

Serves 6 (about $^3/_4$–cup servings)

A Kale Challenge

So many friends and students in my cooking classes have told me that they've never tried kale. Which is a shame because, for one thing, kale is loaded with calcium. Many people who once scoffed at the idea of eating kale go on to become enthusiastic kale eaters after trying the following challenge:

For one week, cook half a bunch of kale, or maybe even only a quarter of a bunch, because you're only going to start with VERY small amounts.

Steam it in a little water with sea salt, then chop it into even smaller (tiny) pieces. Serve each member of your family as small an amount as a teaspoon or two. Eat, chew, and applaud yourselves. Sometimes the kids will start by swallowing it whole. That's OK (it's chopped into tiny pieces).

Day 1 or 2 may be the hardest, but keep this up for a full week, and keep the amounts small, no pressure to eat larger amounts. Do this for seven days, and let me know your results. You'll be surprised at what happens if you give this the "good ol' college try."

Sautéed Beans With Onions and Garlic

1 teaspoon sesame or olive oil
1 to 3 cloves fresh sliced garlic
1 large onion
pinch of sea salt or 1 teaspoon soy sauce
1 to 2 pounds washed green beans (Nothing like fresh from the garden!)

Heat a cast-iron skillet on medium-high heat, add oil, garlic, and onions. Add a pinch of salt or the soy sauce and sauté for 2 to 3 minutes or until garlic is translucent. Add the green beans and another pinch of salt. Sauté for another 3 to 4 minutes until the beans are cooked, but still bright green and firm.

Remove from skillet and serve over brown rice, or as a side dish.

Serves 6–8

Variation: If hot and spicy is your preference, try a little hot pepper sesame oil in place of the sesame oil.

Note: Many people make the mistake of oversalting. In most cases, less is more.

Oven-Roasted Veggies

These oven-roasted veggies are hard for just about anyone to resist and so darned easy to prepare. You can experiment and create your own winning combinations.

Preheat oven to 400 degrees.

I go through phases where I'm just in the mood for certain veggies. This is a combo I currently like a lot: parsnips, carrots, thinly sliced burdock, mushrooms, and beets. Roast whatever you like best.

In a bowl, toss chopped veggies with a little olive oil and sprinkle with sea salt. Make sure to coat evenly. (You'll want to toss the beets separately as their color will seep onto everything!)

Spread vegetables evenly on a cookie sheet and bake until crispy, about 30 minutes.

Simmer-Down Onions

These are great over a baked potato or brown rice. Try them instead of butter or sour cream!

> 1 teaspoon olive or sesame oil
> 2 large onions, cut in half, sliced into half-moon pieces
> 1/4 teaspoon sea salt

In a skillet, heat oil on high, add the onion and salt and stir-fry for a few minutes, still on high. Reduce heat to low, cover, and simmer for 20 minutes or longer if desired. Add a little water if needed.

Serves 4–6

Baked Delicate Delicata

Delicata squash is delicious any way you slice it. Delicata, acorn, and butternut are three of my favorite varieties of squash. For delicata, wash it, cut it in half from top to bottom, then scoop out the seeds from each half with a spoon and slice into half-inch pieces. This squash is delicious simply steamed in a little water.

    1 large delicata squash, thinly sliced

    2 tablespoons brown rice syrup

    1 tablespoon olive oil

    1 tablespoon tamari wheat–free soy sauce

    $1/4$ teaspoon sea salt

    $1/4$ cup walnuts or pecans

Preheat oven to 350 degrees.

Spread the thinly sliced squash on a lightly greased baking sheet (I use olive oil), and drizzle a couple of tablespoons of brown rice syrup over the pieces. Sprinkle with a tablespoon of olive oil, tamari sauce, and then with the sea salt. Top with chopped walnuts or pecans and bake about 30 minutes.

Serves 3–4

Rosti for One

I first heard Heather Mills speak in 2003 at The Amputee Coalition of America's annual conference in Boston. Like me, she has just one leg. My left leg was amputated above the knee because of bone cancer when I was 33, and Heather lost her leg below the knee in 1993, when she was hit by a police motorcycle on an emergency call. Since that tragedy, she has become quite an advocate for amputees, and she has devoted her life to many other causes and charities. She and I have something else in common—we both follow a healthy diet. We've never met in person, but when I needed an advocate for some of my amputee issues, I emailed her and she has been very kind and helpful. Heather owns a famous vegan restaurant in the United Kingdom called VBites (where I hope to dine one day). This recipe from there is smashing!

> 1 whole potato
> $1/2$ carrot, peeled
> $1/2$ parsnip, peeled
> lemon juice to taste
> chopped parsley
> salt and pepper
> olive oil

Preheat oven to 350 degrees.

Grate the potato, carrot, and parsnip into a bowl of water with lemon juice. Drain off the water and wring out the grated vegetables until dry.

Put the vegetables back in the bowl and add chopped parsley, salt, pepper, and olive oil.

Lightly oil a 6-inch pan and place ingredients in the pan. Flatten down, then put into oven. Bake 30 to 40 minutes or until brown. Allow to cool for a few minutes before enjoying.

Serves 1

Break-Down Daikon

Daikon is a radish that looks like a white carrot. Eaten raw, it has a spicy taste. It can be grated and eaten with soy sauce. It is said to break down fat in the body. It can also upset your stomach, so it's best not to eat too much of it.

A Korean friend once told me, "In the American diet, you only have build-up foods like meat and cheese. We have breakdown foods: daikon, cabbage, leeks, scallions, etc." Daikon helps the body burn fat. A word of caution, though! This does not mean that you want to eat this dish every day! Our American way of thinking sometimes leads us to believe that more is better—"Oh, a fat-burning dish?! I want MORE." Not so. Once a week (or twice if you have them growing in your yard) is fine. Enjoy, but don't overdo. Eat a wide variety of fresh (organic, if possible) vegetables.

> **washed daikon, with the tops**
> **water**
> ¹/₂ **teaspoon soy sauce**

Cut the white root (what we consider the daikon) on a diagonal into half-inch slices. Put in a saucepan with ¹/₂ to 1 inch of water, depending on how many you're cooking.
Bring to a boil, cover, reduce heat to medium-low and cook for 2 to 3 minutes.

Chop the washed tops into ¹/₂- to 1-inch pieces. Add some of these to the same pot. Add a little more water if necessary, cover, return to a boil, then reduce heat to low and simmer for 3 more minutes.

Add soy sauce and simmer for 3 more minutes, or until the root is soft but firm. Try it. You'll be pleasantly surprised.

Dried Daikon Fat-Burner

This dish is said to help burn fat in the body and be good for the lymph system because of the dried daikon. It's kind of exotic and one of my daughter's favorites.

6-ounce package of dried daikon (I use Eden brand), soaked in water and reconstituted
3 to 4 dried shiitake mushrooms, soaked in water and reconstituted and sliced
soaking water from the shiitakes and daikon
1 onion, cut into half-moon slices
2 tablespoons of mirin
2 tablespoons of soy sauce
1 teaspoon sesame or other oil

Heat oil in a cast-iron or stainless-steel skillet over medium-high heat. Add onion and sauté for 2 to 3 minutes.

Add the reconstituted daikon and shiitake and sauté for another 3 to 4 minutes. Add enough of the soaking water to the skillet to half-cover the daikon, onion, and shiitake. Turn heat to high to bring to a boil, then reduce to low. Simmer, covered, for 40 minutes.

During the last 10 minutes, add the mirin and soy sauce and continue cooking uncovered to cook off any extra liquid. I prefer a little liquid left in the pan so that this dish is not completely dry.

Serve warm or at room temperature. This stores well in the refrigerator for up to three days. To reuse, take out of refrigerator an hour or so before eating. No need to reheat!

Serves 8–10

Blanched Veggies

Blanched vegetables are quickly cooked by plunging them in hot water for a minute or so. They make a nice addition to practically any meal. Eating lots of vegetables, some fruit, and cutting out animal protein (when your body digests animal protein, it produces more heat) is a good way to cool your body when it's hot.

  1 bunch kale, washed and sliced thinly
  5 medium carrots, washed, sliced thinly on a diagonal
  2 stalks broccoli, washed and cut, stalks peeled and sliced thinly
  4 large handfuls (4 cups) green beans, washed, with ends removed
  (any fresh vegetables will work, sliced thinly and cut about the same size)

Fill a pot half full with spring or filtered tap water. Bring to a rolling boil over medium-high heat.

 Place each vegetable, one type at a time, in the water. Boil uncovered only until the color turns bright—a minute or less—then remove using a fine-mesh skimmer.

Drain each vegetable on a flat surface to stop cooking.

Blanch each type of vegetable in order from mildest- to strongest-tasting so that each retains its distinct flavor and color.

Blanched vegetables can be served any number of ways: plain, with dressing, or with a splash of vinegar or lemon juice. They can be served warm, at room temperature, or chilled; tossed together, or arranged in sections on a platter.

Serves about 12

Raise-the-Roof Sweet Potato– Vegetable Lasagna

Rip Esselstyn is the creator of the hugely popular 28-day Engine 2 Diet, a nutritional program that helps people lower cholesterol and lose weight. I remember hearing about his The Engine 2 Diet *when Whole Foods CEO John Mackey called it his favorite book. That piqued my interest and I was pleased to learn that Rip promotes a plant-based diet. His father is Dr. Caldwell B. Esselstyn Jr., who wrote an amazing, hopeful book about reversing heart disease through diet, and his grandfather and great-grandfather were also well-known physicians. Rip, a former world-class triathlete and an Austin, Texas, (Engine 2 Station) firefighter, offers this favorite.*

> 1 large onion, chopped
> 1 small head garlic, all cloves chopped or pressed
> 8 ounces mushrooms, sliced
> 1 head broccoli, chopped, without stems
> 2 large carrots, chopped
> 2 red bell peppers, seeded and chopped
> 1 (15-ounce) can corn, rinsed and drained
> 1 (16-ounce) package firm tofu
> 1/2 teaspoon cayenne pepper
> 1 teaspoon oregano, preferably fresh
> 1 teaspoon basil, preferably fresh
> 1 teaspoon rosemary, preferably fresh
> 2 (25-ounce) jars pasta sauce (I like Muir Glen Organic Italian-herbed and
>   Organic Garlic Roasted)
> 2 (8-ounce) boxes whole-grain lasagna noodles, uncooked
> 16 ounces frozen spinach, thawed and drained
> 2 sweet potatoes, cooked and mashed
> 6 Roma tomatoes, sliced thinly
> 1 cup raw cashews, ground

Preheat oven to 400 degrees.

Sauté the onions and garlic on high heat for 3 minutes in a wok or non-stick pan. Add the mushrooms and cook until onions are limp and mushrooms release their liquid. Remove them to a large bowl using a slotted spoon. Reserve mushroom liquid in the pan.

Sauté the broccoli and carrots for 5 minutes and add to the mushroom bowl. Sauté the peppers and corn until just beginning to soften. Add to the bowl of vegetables. Drain tofu by wrapping in paper towels. Break it up directly into the towel and combine with the vegetable mixture. Add spices to the bowl of vegetables and combine.

To assemble: Cover the bottom of a 9- x 13-inch casserole with a layer of sauce. Add a layer of noodles. Cover the noodles with sauce. This way the noodles cook in the oven rather than being boiled first, saving time and energy. Spread the vegetable mixture over the sauce-covered noodles. Cover with a layer of noodles and another dressing of sauce.

Add the spinach to the second layer of sauced noodles. Cover the spinach with the mashed sweet potatoes. Add another layer of sauce, the final layer of noodles, and a last topping of sauce. Cover the lasagna with thinly sliced Roma tomatoes, then cover the dish with foil and bake for 45 minutes.

Remove foil, sprinkle the top with ground cashews, and return to oven for 15 minutes. Let sit for 15 minutes before serving.

Serves 10–12

Vegetable Stir-Fry with Tofu

2 teaspoons sesame oil

$1/4$ head cabbage, thinly sliced

8 ounces organic tofu (I use organic tofu to avoid GMOs—genetically modified organisms), cut into small cubes

3 carrots, thinly sliced on a diagonal

3 ribs of celery, thinly sliiced on a diagonal

2 or 3 collard green leaves, sliced into thin ribbons

$1/8$ teaspoon of sea salt (I use SI brand)

1 tablespoon juice from freshly grated ginger

1 or 2 green onions, sliced thinly on a diagonal

Heat oil in a cast-iron skillet over medium-high heat. Add cabbage, stir-fry for 1 to 2 minutes. Add tofu, carrots, celery, collards, and sea salt and stir-fry until slightly wilted and soft, but still colorful, about 5 minutes. Add ginger juice and garnish with green onions.

Serve over brown rice (see Amazingly-Good-For-You Brown Rice, p. 19), or brown rice noodles.

Serves 3–4

Napa Cabbage

Cooked Napa cabbage still looks vibrant. Napa contains no fat or cholesterol, is low in calories and sodium, and high in vitamin C.

Napa cabbage is a brassica vegetable. These aid in the prevention of cancer. If you've never eaten greens, this is a good one to start with because of its mild flavor. Napa cabbage is delicious. When quickly steamed or blanched, it has a natural buttery taste. It makes an excellent breakfast green because of its lightness and slight crunchiness. I get mine at the farmers' market in Portland, Maine. I occasionally add Napa to stir-frys, or make a pressed salad with it.

To blanch: Fill a pot with filtered water and bring to a boil over high heat. Add chopped or shredded Napa cabbage to the pot. Leave it in for 1 minute, drain, and put it into a bowl and serve as a side dish.

To steam: Fill a pot with a small amount of water (¼ cup), add chopped or shredded Napa cabbage. Bring to a boil over high heat, cover, reduce heat to low, and simmer for 1 to 2 minutes. Drain, put into a bowl, and serve as a side dish.

Summery Stir-Fry Side

1 teaspoon sesame oil
3 carrots, sliced thinly on a diagonal
pinch of sea salt
1 large handful green beans
1 large handful Dragon's Lingerie beans (look for these Dutch heirloom wax beans
    at the farmers' market)
optional: 1 tablespoon mirin

Heat sesame oil in a cast-iron skillet over high heat. Add carrots, mirin (if using), and sea salt and sauté for 2 to 3 minutes. Add both types of beans and continue sautéing for 3 to 4 more minutes, or until the beans are slightly soft, but the green beans are still a vibrant green.

Serves 3–4 as a side dish

For water sautéing: Sprinkle a few teaspoons of water onto the hot skillet and sauté as above.

Cozy Kuzu Veggies

Kuzu is the same thing as kudzu. It's a root starch that is soothing to the stomach.

1 to 2 teaspoons sesame oil
1/2 onion, diced
pinch of sea salt
1 carrot, thinly sliced
1/2 cup cauliflower, chopped
1/2 cup broccoli, chopped
1 teaspoon kuzu powder, dissolved in 1/4 to 1/2 cup water
optional: toasted almonds

Add oil, onions, and salt to a hot skillet on high flame and sauté for 1 to 2 minutes. Add carrot, cauliflower, broccoli, and almonds (if using), and sauté for 4 to 5 more minutes. Add diluted kuzu and stir until it's thickened (add more water if too thick). Cook for another 1 to 2 minutes on low to medium heat. Serve over a whole grain. This saves well and can be eaten as leftovers.

Serves 1–2

Beet Slaw with Blueberry Vinaigrette

Dr. Lisa Belisle contacted me a few years ago, after reading my book Becoming Whole. She was also a follower of my blog and was starting one herself. We have a mutual interest in helping people eat better and we've become friends. Lisa is gorgeous, sincere, and earnest. She's very humble. She's also a doctor specializing in integrative medicine and acupuncture. And she's a writer and a mom! She also does a lot of volunteer work for Safe Passage, an organization started by the late Hanley Denning (Lisa's longtime friend and roommate at Bowdoin College) to help poor children who scavenge food from garbage dumps in Guatemala. Lisa is an extremely well-rounded and delightful woman. She has many talents, including cooking. She loves beets, and you'll love her beet recipe.

Blueberry Vinaigrette

1 to 2 teaspoons olive oil, for sautéing

1 or 2 shallots, peeled and finely chopped

2 tablespoons extra virgin olive oil

2 tablespoons blueberry vinegar

2 tablespoons apple cider vinegar

juice from one lemon

$1/4$ teaspoon salt

$1/4$ teaspoon pepper or to taste

Slaw

$1/2$ cup shredded carrots

1 cup shredded golden beets

1 cup shredded purple cabbage

2 cups shredded red beets

Heat olive oil in a saucepan over medium heat. Add shallots. Sauté until translucent, approximately 3 to 5 minutes. Allow to cool. Combine with other dressing ingredients in a blender or food processor. Process until smooth.

Combine slaw ingredients and fold into the vinaigrette. Place in a festive bowl and refrigerate for at least half an hour before serving to allow the flavors to blend.

Serves 6

Note: Keep shredded beets separate from other slaw ingredients until just before adding vinaigrette. Beet pigment has a tendency to "bleed" onto surrounding foods (and porous food-preparation surfaces, such as wood).

Garnish with minced parsley, sesame seeds, or chopped, toasted walnuts.

Best Sweet Cabbage

Cabbage belongs to the Cruciferae family of vegetables, along with kale, broccoli, collards, and Brussels sprouts. Cabbage is an excellent source of vitamin C and many other nutrients. Cruciferous vegetables also contain substances that promote detoxification of the blood and tissues and help to fight cancer. Try this on St. Patrick's Day!

    1/4 cup extra virgin olive oil
    1 head green cabbage, sliced thinly
    1 cup water
    2 tablespoons mirin
    1 tablespoon soy sauce
    2 tablespoons tahini (I like Maranatha Organic No-Salt Added Raw Sesame Tahini)
    2 tablespoons rice syrup (try Lundberg Organic)
    1/4 cup raisins (dark or golden)
    1/4 cup parsley, fresh chopped
    1 (8-ounce package) vegetable tempeh (organic, if possible, no GMOs)
    1/2 teaspoon sea salt

In a 5-quart stainless-steel soup pot, add the olive oil and cabbage. Turn heat to high. After oil is heated, reduce heat to medium-high and sauté the cabbage for 5 to 10 minutes.

Add water, mirin, soy sauce, tahini, rice syrup, raisins, tempeh, and sea salt. Bring back to a boil over high heat. Cover, reduce heat to low, and simmer for 30 minutes, stirring occasionally. If liquid reduces during cooking, add a little more water to prevent burning. Serve garnished with parsley.

Serves 4–6

Glazed Brussels Sprouts

Think you don't like Brussels sprouts? I'm confident this recipe will change your mind forever.

Glaze

> ¹/₈ **cup apple juice**
> ¹/₈ **cup water**
> **pinch of salt or 1 teaspoon soy sauce**
> **1 tablespoon brown rice syrup**

Cut 10 washed Brussels sprouts into halves or quarters, depending on their size. Heat olive or sesame oil in a cast-iron skillet over medium-high heat. Add the cut-up Brussels sprouts and sauté for 2 to 3 minutes. Add ¹/₄ cup water. Cover, reduce heat to low, and simmer for 3 to 5 minutes.

Mix the glaze ingredients in a measuring cup or small bowl and whisk together. Remove the skillet cover, add the glaze, and cook for 3 more minutes. Serve warm.

Serves 2–3

Long, Slow-Steamed Vegetables

This is a nice way to cook a variety of cold-weather vegetables for any occasion. I use a combination of whatever I have on hand. For special get-togethers, I sometimes add a dash of apple juice to the cooking water, which brings out the sweetness of the vegetables. If there's room, I add greens to the top the pan during the last 3 minutes of cooking.

> 2- to 3 -inch strip kombu, soaked and sliced into small strips
> 1/4 cup daikon, sliced into large chunks
> 1 onion, sliced into large wedges
> 1/4 cabbage, cut into large wedges
> 1/4 cup hard, sweet winter squash, cubed
> 1 carrot, cut into large chunks
> *optional:* also include burdock or lotus root, but cut them smaller than the other vegetables)
> 3 to 4 drops soy sauce
> 1/2 cup water for steaming

Place kombu and its soaking water in the bottom of a pot. Layer vegetables on top of one another in the following order: daikon, onion, cabbage, squash, and carrot.

Cover the pot and bring to a boil over medium-high heat until there's steam coming from the pot. Reduce heat and cook without disturbing pot for 15 to 20 minutes, or longer. If the water evaporates during cooking, add more to the pot. When the vegetables are tender, add a few drops of soy sauce and mix. Replace cover and simmer for 5 more minutes. Remove from heat, let sit, and serve after a couple minutes.

Serves 6

Other combinations you might try: turnip, onion, carrot, shiitake mushroom • carrot, leek, cauliflower, corn, daikon, shiitake, daikon greens • burdock, carrot, onion, squash

Skillet Cabbage Lunch

There are no ingredients listed for this recipe because you can do this with practically any-thing that seems appealing together. This is so typical of what I do for lunch. I cut up carrots, celery, purple cabbage, and thinly sliced collards, sauté them in a little hot-pepper sesame oil, and throw in some leftover cooked quinoa and a pinch of salt or teaspoon of olive oil.

Be creative and see what combos work for you. Garnish with some chopped scallion, maybe a handful of toasted pumpkin seeds. Steam a little broccoli to have with it, and you are all set with a simple, fast, and nutritious lunch or dinner—or even breakfast.

Eating healthy doesn't have to be difficult!

Roasted Roots

Hard not to love them!

1 sweet potato
2 parsnips
2 carrots
2 turnips or 1 large rutabaga
1 daikon
2 or 3 tablespoons olive oil
optional: substitute/add in your favorites, like squash
1 teaspoon salt
dash of pepper
optional herbs: rosemary, thyme, or sage (fresh if possible)

Pre-heat oven to 375 degrees.

Wash and chop all vegetables into large bite-size pieces. Place in a large baking dish with sides. Drizzle with olive oil then mix well to coat each vegetable lightly with the oil. Sprinkle with salt, pepper to taste, and herbs.

Bake uncovered for 25 to 35 minutes until vegetables are tender and golden brown, checking every 10 minutes to stir and make sure the veggies are not sticking.

Serves 4–6

Note: Any combination of vegetables will work. Roasting only one kind of vegetable also makes a nice side dish.

Carrot, Burdock, and Shiitake Kinpira

Kinpira, a traditional macrobiotic (and Japanese) dish revered for its strengthening qualities, is sautéed over high heat, then simmered. I ate this a few times a week when I first started my healing diet, and I still really like it. Burdock is a vegetable that strengthens the body and purifies the blood.

2 large carrots, sliced into matchstick pieces
2 pieces burdock root, sliced into matchstick pieces
4 shiitake mushrooms, sliced thinly
1 to 2 teaspoons sesame oil
1 ¼ cups water
1 to 2 teaspoons soy sauce
optional: wheat-free tamari or 1 teaspoon ginger juice can also be used
1 tablespoon mirin

Heat oil on medium to high heat and sauté the vegetables, stirring for 5 minutes. Add water, soy sauce (or tamari or ginger juice), and mirin, turn heat to low, cover. Simmer 15 more minutes. Water will cook down, but check water level to prevent burning.

Serves 6–8.

Colleen's Stir-Fry

This tasty and colorful combination is from my friend Colleen Taintor. We enjoyed this the first time with a fresh corn salad, a rice salad, and some leftover cranberry beans.

2 small yellow summer squash, sliced thinly
2 small zucchini, sliced thinly
$1/4$ bunch of curly leaf kale, sliced thinly
$1/4$ head cauliflower
1 to 2 teaspoons olive oil
pinch of sea salt
3 or 4 caramelized onions
pepper to taste

To caramelize onions: Cut 3 (or more) large onions in half and slice into half-moon pieces. Put skillet on medium-high heat, add 1 tablespoon olive oil and a few pinches of sea salt. When the skillet gets hot, reduce heat to low and sauté the onions for 5 to 10 minutes or longer. I find the longer I sauté the onions, the sweeter they get.

To make stir-fry: Heat a skillet on high, add olive oil, then vegetables. Add pinches of sea salt. Lightly stir-fry for 3 to 5 minutes.

Serves 3–4

Whipped Sweets

When sweet potatoes are cooking on a cold Maine day, they fill the kitchen with warmth and a heavenly aroma. And then even more of a treat: Whipped Sweets.

3 large sweet potatoes, about 3 pounds
2 tablespoons olive oil
1 teaspoon sea salt
1/4 cup apple juice
1 tablespoon brown rice syrup
2 tablespoons maple syrup

Preheat oven to 400 degrees.

Place sweet potatoes on a baking sheet and roast until easily pierced with a fork, about 1 hour.

Peel the skin off the sweet potatoes while still hot. By hand or with a mixer, mash or whip the potatoes until all large chunks are gone. Combine potatoes, olive oil, salt, apple juice, brown rice syrup, and maple syrup in a large bowl. Continue to mix together until all lumps are gone. Adjust seasonings to your specific tastes.

Serves 6–8

Note: These can be made the day before and reheated.

Sweet Turnips with Maple Glaze

This could be made with brown rice syrup for another flavor.

3 average-size turnips, with skins, washed and chopped into ¹/₂-inch squares
pinch of sea salt

Maple Glaze

¹/₃ cup organic apple cider, or apple juice (I like Ricker Hill Orchards)
pinch of sea salt
1 tablespoon organic maple syrup (I like Stawberry Hill Farm)
dash of cinnamon
1 teaspoon kuzu or arrowroot

In a small pot with a lid, add the turnips and sea salt with enough water to cover and bring to a boil on high. Reduce heat to low, cover, and simmer for 10 minutes.

In a small bowl, add apple cider, sea salt, maple syrup. Add kuzu and stir to dilute. Set the mixture aside.

Heat a small cast-iron skillet on high, add 1 tablespoon of olive oil. Remove coooked turnips from the pot and add to the skillet. Stir glaze and add to skillet, heat and stir slowly 1 minute until glaze thickens and coats the turnips.

Serves 6

Make-Juice-Not-War Green Juice

I first heard about Kris Carr, author, filmmaker, self-proclaimed "wellness warrior" and animal rights activist, through a friend at the Cancer Community Center in South Portland, Maine, where I taught cooking classes. The center had an ad in its flier about Kris coming to speak in Portland, and a blurb about her film, Crazy Sexy Cancer. In her documentary, Kris reveals that she was an active young woman who was diagnosed with an "incurable," mysterious, and rare type of cancer that did not respond to any conventional treatments. She went beyond the conventional, and started experimenting with food. She's now a wellness maven with a popular enterprise called Crazy Sexy Life, which is helping so many people. A few years ago, we wound up sitting next to each other by chance at an event in New York City. Kris is radiant! The motto that she lives by, "Make juice, not war," is also the name of her favorite breakfast juice. Enjoy!

> 2 large cucumbers (peeled if not organic)
> 4 stalks kale
> 4 or 5 romaine leaves
> 4 stalks celery
> 1 or 2 large broccoli stems
> 1 or 2 pears
> 1 inch ginger root (or less)
> *other optional greens:* parsley, spinach, and dandelion
> add sweet pea or sunflower sprouts when available

Just cut it all up and throw it in a blender.

Makes 32 ounces

Broccoli Salad with Creamy Mustard Dressing

Christy Morgan is picking up the torch—doing her part to help spread the message to a younger generation that what we eat matters most. I first met Christy online through my son, Francis. He met her while living in Los Angeles a few years ago because she made and delivered macrobiotic meals, and Francis follows a very healthy diet. Our whole family later met this interesting young woman, who now teaches cooking classes in Los Angeles. What she calls a macrobiotic and raw fusion, I call yummy! Christy maintains a blog called The Blissful Chef, with lots of helpful information and great food photos. Here is one of her favorite dishes.

   1 large crown of broccoli, cut into florets, tough parts removed from stem, chopped
   1 carrot, grated
   1 can chickpeas, washed and drained
   2 red radishes, thinly sliced

Creamy Mustard Dressing

   $1/2$ cup mayonnaise (vegan recommended)
   2 tablespoons Dijon mustard
   zest of 1 lemon
   1 tablespoon maple syrup
   1 tablespoon apple cider vinegar
   pinch of black pepper

Steam the broccoli until crisp-tender, about 2 minutes. Remove from heat and toss with the remainder of the salad ingredients. Whisk together the dressing ingredients in a small bowl. Toss with the salad and chill for 10 minutes before serving. It's great the next day, too!

Serves 2–4

Vegetable Pot-Stickers

Arame is mild, sweet-flavored, mineral-rich brown algae.

1 package wonton wrappers
5 cups safflower oil
$1/4$ round green cabbage, sliced thinly
pinch of sea salt
1 large carrot, grated
4 shiitake mushrooms, thinly sliced
$1/8$ cup water
$1/3$ package (1.75-ounce package) arame sea vegetable, reconstituted
1 tablespoon good-quality soy sauce
1 tablespoon mirin
$1/4$ cup fresh ginger juice (grate, squeeze out juice, discard pulp)
2 scallions, thinly sliced

Dipping Sauce

1 scallion, sliced
$1/2$ cup soy sauce
$1/4$ cup rice vinegar
1 or 2 teaspoons fresh ginger juice (grate, squeeze out juice, discard pulp)

To make filling: In a cast-iron skillet, heat 1 tablespoon of the oil on high, but watch closely. Add the cabbage and salt and stir-fry for 1 minute. Add the carrot and shiitakes. Fry for 3 to 4 minutes. Add $1/8$ cup of water, arame, soy sauce, and mirin. Bring to a boil, reduce heat to low, and simmer for 2 more minutes. Add the ginger juice and garnish with scallions. Let cool.

To fill: Place the wonton wrappers, a small bowl of water, and the cooled filling on the countertop. Take one wrapper and place a tablespoon of filling in the middle. Dip your finger in water and dot half the wrapper (these are floured so it makes a glue). Lightly fold and press together, not too hard. (If I'm feeling creative, I'll crimp and scallop the edges.) Do this until you run out of wrappers or filling.

To cook: In a soup pot, heat the remaining oil on high until it is almost boiling, about 4 minutes. Don't let the oil get so hot that it smokes. Reduce heat to medium. Gently add 1 pot-sticker and fry for 1 to 2 minutes until crispy. Remove from oil with a slotted spoon and place on paper towels on a platter. Fry no more than four pot-stickers at a time.

Dipping sauce: Cook soy sauce and vinegar on medium for 5 minutes. Add ginger juice and scallions, stir, and enjoy.

Makes approximately 3 dozen.

Note: The oil can be refrigerated and used again within a week.

Oven-Roasted Jewel Yams with Pecans

These are definitely a holiday favorite. Such a great alternative to the marshmallow-brown sugar variety.

3 jewel yams (or sweet potatoes), sliced into half-rounds
$1/4$ cup toasted pecan halves (whole)
3 tablespoons brown rice syrup
2 tablespoons olive oil
$1/2$ teaspoon sea salt

Preheat oven to 375 degrees.

Grease a cookie sheet with a thin layer of olive oil.

Arrange the yams or sweet potatoes on the sheet so that they fit (overlapping slightly if needed). Place a toasted pecan half on each slice. Drizzle small amounts of brown rice syrup over each piece. Repeat with the olive oil. Sprinkle with sea salt. Roast for 40 minutes.

Serves 6

Craving Sugar

Sugar cravings are not the easiest thing to shake. Here are some steps to help you beat that urge to reach for something sugary:

1. Make sure you don't have too much salt and animal protein in your diet. Salt and protein make your body contract and tighten, while sugar makes your body relax, or loosen up. An overabundance of salt causes the body to crave the opposite: sugar.

2. Eat more vegetables. Try to experiment with new vegetables that you haven't had before. If you don't like them, try small amounts at a sitting . . . even as little as a bite or two. Vegetables relax the body (like sugar) and are high in nutrients and fiber.

3. Eat brown rice (or another whole grain) once or twice a day. Unlike sugar, a complex carbohydrate keeps your blood sugar (and your moods) stable for longer periods of time. And they keep you satiated longer, too.

4. Have a piece of fruit for dessert. Or, have a cooked fruit dessert a couple times a week.

5. Get enough rest. I know there aren't enough hours in a day . . . so begin the good habit of prioritizing. What's most important? For me, it's my health. Try going to bed earlier.

6. Self reflect. Is there something in your life that's causing you stress—something that you may be numbing out with sugar? Don't be afraid to ask for help if you need it. (Seeking help is a sign of strength, not weakness.)

7. Relax . . . take more time to nurture yourself. Find the "sweetness" in life, be it a hobby, visiting friends for tea, or just making time to sit peacefully in your back yard.

soups

Soups are an easy way to start eating healthy. When I began eating better, I followed recipes to a T. I used the exact ingredients and amounts a recipe called for, as this seemed necessary starting out. I had never used some of these ingredients before and I wanted to get it right. Today, I'm more relaxed and usually make up my own recipes.

Soups are great because they can be made ahead of time, frozen if necessary, and they're economical—and a great way to use up leftovers, especially beans. I frequently have a bean dish for dinner one day and it becomes soup the next day—with a lot of fresh vegetables and a garnish added.

Glistening Squash and Carrot Ginger Soup

1 medium winter squash, cubed (Leave skin on if butternut is used. If kabocha or other green squash is used, peel skin, so as not to have green soup!)
6 large carrots, sliced
1 medium onion, sliced
4 cups water to cover veggies
1-inch piece of ginger, grated for juice
sea salt, or tamari, to taste

Sauté the onion in olive oil or water over medium-high heat for 1 to 2 minutes. Cut up the squash and carrots and combine with the onions in a soup pot. Add just enough water to cover the vegetables and bring to a boil. Add a small pinch of sea salt. Cover, reduce heat to low, and simmer for 30 minutes until the squash is soft.

Mash the squash with a potato masher right in the pot, or use a food processor to puree. Add another pinch of sea salt (or teaspoon of soy sauce). Simmer for 7 to 10 more minutes. Serve hot, garnished with fresh parsley and a little juice from grated ginger.

Serves 4

Pleasing Pea Soup

Split pea soup is one of my all-time favorite comfort foods. I think this is because of the creamy texture and flavorful, fresh ingredients. I love it served piping hot with a bowl of rice or a slice of whole-grain bread. It's one of my quick and easy meals. If you add 4 ounces of chopped tempeh (while simmering for 30 minutes), you can make it a one-pot meal!

We also like to have this soup with Tom's fried rice and a plethora of steamed veggies —cauliflower, green beans, broccoli, and kale. I often have the leftovers for lunch.

1 cup split peas
1-inch strip wakame (sea vegetable) or kombu
1/8 cup burdock, diced into very small pieces
1 onion, diced
optional: 1 clove garlic
5 or 6 cups water
1 carrot or parsnip, diced
1 stalk celery, diced
1 tablespoon tamari (wheat-free) soy sauce
1/2 teaspoon each dried oregano and sweet basil

Wash peas several times until the water is clear. Add sea vegetable, burdock, onion, and garlic if desired. Add enough water to cover by 1 inch. Bring to a boil on high heat, cover, reduce heat to low, and simmer for 30 minutes.

Add other veggies and just enough water to make desired creaminess, simmer for 30 minutes. Add soy sauce, oregano, and basil in the last 10 minutes.

Serves 4

Make-You-Strong Stew

2 cups dried adzuki beans, soaked overnight, rinsed, and drained
1 large onion, diced
1 teaspoon olive or sesame oil
4 dried shiitake mushrooms, soaked in water to soften and sliced thinly
1 large rutabaga, cut in medium-large pieces
optional: parsnips or potatoes, cut into small cubes
1 1/2 to 2 tablespoons miso paste (1- to 3-year aged miso is best)
1/2 cup chopped parsley

Add oil to a large soup pot, and heat on medium-high heat. Add the onion and cook for 3 to 5 minutes, or until soft. Add the beans and enough water to cover the beans (about 6 cups). Cover and bring to a boil.

Reduce heat to low and simmer for 45 minutes, or until the beans are tender, adding a little more hot water if necessary.

Add 6 more cups of water, return the soup to a boil, then reduce heat back to simmer. Add shiitakes, rutabaga (and potatoes or parsnips, if using), cover, and cook for 30 more minutes.

Dilute the miso paste in a little water and add to the soup, cook on low for 5 to 10 more minutes. Garnish with chopped parsley.

Serves 6–8

Sweet & Sour Kidney Bean Soup

2 cups cooked kidney beans (Maine grown are the best)

4 cups water or vegetable broth

1 cup Napa or green cabbage, cut into small cubes

1 large carrot, cut into large cubes

2 ribs celery, diced

1 small onion, diced

1 whole onion

optional: 1/4 cup frozen organic corn

3 dried shiitake mushrooms, reconstituted in water, thinly sliced

1/8 cup apple butter (I like Pastor Chuck's brand, with no sugar, and from Maine, too)

1 teaspoon grain mustard

2 teaspoons soy sauce (or tamari, wheat-free soy sauce), 1/2 teaspoon of sea salt,
    or 2 teaspoons miso

2 tablespoons fresh lemon juice

chopped green onions as a garnish

optional: fresh rosemary or other spices

Place the cooked kidney beans and water or broth in a soup pot and bring to a boil on high. Add the vegetables. When the pot returns to a boil, reduce heat to low and simmer for 45 minutes. During this time remove 1/2 cup of broth from the pot and add the apple butter, mustard, and fresh rosemary, and stir together, then return it to the soup pot.

During the last 10 minutes of cooking, add the soy sauce, sea salt, or miso. When finished cooking, add the fresh lemon juice. Garnish with chopped green onions.

Serve with Homemade Croutons (p. 92), and/or a bowl of warm grain, such as brown rice, millet, or barley.

Serves 6–8

Homemade Croutons

The crowning glory and an excellent way to use day-old bread.

> ¹/₂ to 1 loaf of bread, cut into 1-inch cubes (I use Black Crow Bakery or Mother's
>   Oven breads)
> 2 to 3 tablespoons olive oil
> pinch of sea salt
> *optional:* Dried herbs (I sometimes use "The Blend," from The Maine Accent—
>   a combination of parsley, basil, marjoram, chervil, garlic, and spices)

Cover the bottom of a cast-iron skillet with olive or other oil. Heat on medium-high. Add cubes of bread and cook, stirring occasionally to prevent burning. Cook the bread until browned. When pan gets very hot, reduce heat to low. When the croutons are browned and toasted, add sea salt (and other herbs if desired). Serve a small portion of croutons with any soup.

Navy Bean Soup

This recipe shows how simple it is to use leftover beans. It doesn't need to be difficult to be easy, healthy, and delicious!

> 2 cups cooked white beans (Leftover or canned may be used occasionally)
> 1 tablespoon barley malt or ¹/₄ cup sugarless apple butter
> ¹/₂ package, or 4 ounces of tempeh, cut into squares
> 1 onion, diced
> 1 sprig rosemary, chopped
> 1 large carrot, diced
> ¹/₂ teaspoon sea salt
> 6 cups water
> ¹/₂ cup chopped parsley

Put all the ingredients (except the parsley) into a soup pot. Bring to a boil over high heat, reduce heat to low, cover, and simmer, stirring occasionally, for 30 to 40 minutes. Add parsley and stir.

Serves 6

Mighty-Good Minestrone

This is a family favorite, especially with simple-to-make Homemade Croutons (p. 92).

- 1 cup cannellini beans (white Italian kidney beans)
- 1 cup kidney beans
- 1 cup lentils
- 10 cups water
- 1 onion
- 3 carrots, diced
- $^1/_2$ pound green beans (in season)
- 3 stalks celery, diced
- 1 cup frozen or fresh corn
- 1 cup fresh parsley, chopped
- 1 $^1/_2$ cups uncooked rice pasta or other pasta
- $^1/_4$ cup ume plum vinegar
- 1-inch piece of kombu
- 1 bouillon cube (vegan suggested)
- 1 tablespoon olive oil
- *optional:* 1 teaspoon Italian seasoning

Soak the cannellini and kidney beans overnight. Prepare vegetables.

Discard the soaking water and refill pot with water to cover beans by 2 inches. Bring the beans to a boil over high heat, turn to low, cover, and cook for 90 minutes.

Add more water and return to simmer. Add vegetables, bouillon, and oil, and cook for 15 minutes. Add pasta and cook for another 15 minutes. Add ume vinegar and parsley, then stir.

Serve with brown rice and veggies.

Serves 10–12 (or maybe a small army)

Gazpacho

I began eating a plant-based diet based on whole grains, beans, and vegetables in 1999 to help me recover from advanced breast cancer. While living in Bethel, Maine, two years later, I saw a small ad in a local paper by actor Ed Asner, telling about The Cancer Project, a branch of PCRM.org started and maintained by Neal Barnard, M.D., the president of the Physicians Committee for Responsible Medicine. PCRM.org had a wealth of helpful information that backed up what I was trying.

Having just started teaching cooking classes, I also found useful info there to pass on to my students. I became a PCRM member because I felt that Neal and his staff were really working hard with their research and with educating people about plant-based diets at a time when little else was being done. In 2004, The Cancer Project started certifying cooks to teach healthy vegan cooking classes, and I earned this certification in the winter 2009-10. PCRM continues to lobby and work tirelessly for healthy school lunches and on education about healing type II diabetes through a plant-based diet. It has also made great strides in stopping animal cruelty. I continue to be a PCRM supporter and I've gotten to know Neal through various fundraisers. Here is one of Dr. Barnard's favorite soups.

> 4 medium ripe tomatoes, diced
> 1 medium cucumber, peeled and diced
> 1 green pepper, seeded and diced
> 1 medium red onion, diced
> 1 clove garlic, crushed
> salt & pepper to taste
> juice of 1 lemon
> 1 or 2 cups tomato juice
> pimentos to taste
> Tabasco sauce to taste
> crumbled cilantro to taste

In a large bowl, combine the diced tomatoes and the next seven ingredients and mix thoroughly. To serve, ladle into individual bowls and add pimentos and Tabasco sauce to taste. Garnish with cilantro.

Serves 2

Neal says: "About twenty years ago, I found myself having dinner in a Paris restaurant. The food was lovely and the staff was friendly. By the end of the meal, I was so taken with the gazpacho that I asked the chef for the recipe. He kindly scratched it down on a napkin."

Hot & Spicy Soup

I usually serve Hot & Spicy Soup to my family with a side of brown rice and steamed broc-coli—because I use the broccoli stems in the soup. Try this soup if you're looking for something healthy that both adults and kids will really like.

1 teaspoon hot pepper sesame oil

2 teaspoons sesame oil

1 large yellow onion, cut in half then thinly sliced into half-moon pieces

4 or 5 dried shiitake mushrooms, soaked to reconstitute, thinly sliced

1 (8-ounce) package button or baby portabella mushrooms, thinly sliced

8 ounces seitan (wheat gluten), sliced thinly, then sliced into matchstick pieces

6 to 8 cups water

2 to 3 broccoli stalks, peeled, sliced into thin coins, then sliced into matchstick pieces

8 ounces tofu, cut into small cubes

1 teaspoon soy sauce

2 tablespoons mirin

1/8 cup kuzu or arrowroot powder, dissolved in 1 cup cold water

1- to 2-inch piece of fresh ginger, finely grated (make into a ball in your palm,
    and squeeze a small amount of juice into each bowl of soup, stir, and serve) 2 to 3
scallions, thinly sliced on a diagonal, for garnish

optional: crushed black pepper

Warm the sesame and hot sesame oil in a soup pot over medium-high heat . Add the onion and sauté for 2 to 3 minutes. Add the mushrooms and sauté for another 2 to 3 minutes. Stir in seitan and add water. Cover, increase heat to high, and bring to a boil. Reduce heat to low and simmer. Stir in the broccoli and tofu, then cover and simmer for 25 to 30 minutes.

Season with soy sauce and mirin and simmer for 10 minutes. Add dissolved kuzu or arrowroot and stir until the soup thickens slightly, about 5 more minutes.

Ladle soup into bowls, squeeze ginger juice into each bowl, and stir. Serve piping hot garnished with scallions. Add a sprinkle of crushed black pepper if desired.

Serves 6–8

Elegant Noodley Broth

This is so nourishing to me, body and soul. Everyone in my family loves this dish, and it's quite easy to put together. It's always a crowd-pleaser.

1 package udon (thick Japanese wheat flour noodles) or soba (thin Japanese wheat flour noodles), cooked according to package directions (I use Tinkyada brand)

10 cups water

2 or 3 shiitake mushrooms, reconstituted in water, thinly sliced

1-inch piece kombu

1 onion, cut in half, then sliced in half-moon pieces

5-inch piece burdock, cut into thin coins, then sliced into matchsticks

1 large carrot, cut in matchsticks

2 stalks celery, sliced finely on a diagonal

8 ounces tofu, cubed

3 tablespoons shoyu

optional: 2 tablespoons mirin

optional: brown rice vinegar

2 tablespoons fresh ginger juice (grate ginger thinly, form into a ball, squeeze juice, and discard the pulp)

optional: Garnish with 1 sheet nori seaweed, cut into rectangles with kitchen scissors, then cut into thin slices, or 3 tablespoons roasted sesame seeds

scallions, sliced thinly on diagonal for garnish

Cook noodles in separate pot per instructions. Drain and set aside.

In a large soup pot bring 10 cups of water to a boil on high heat, then add the kombu and shiitake. Reduce heat to low and simmer for 10 to 20 minutes. Remove the kombu and shiitake, slice both into strips, and return to broth.

Add the onion, burdock, and carrot and simmer for 10 more minutes. Add the celery, tofu, and shoyu (or mirin and a splash of brown rice vinegar). Simmer for 5 more minutes.

Turn off heat, add ginger juice to the soup and stir.

Place the cooked noodles in a serving bowl and ladle hot broth filled with vegetables and tofu cubes over the noodles. Garnish with scallions (or sesame seeds and nori).

Serves 8–10

Creamy Flageolet Bean and Veggie Soup

According to the Gourmet Sleuth, flageolet beans are "small immature kidney beans with a history that dates back to the 1800s in France. They're available fresh, dried, or canned. The bean is available in a variety of colors, including white (flageolet blanc), black (noir), yellow (jaune), red (rouge), or green (vert)." I usually buy the greenish-white dried beans in the bins at Whole Foods.

    3 cups dried flageolet beans, soaked overnight
    1-inch piece of kombu
    3/8 teaspoon sea salt
    1 large carrot, diced
    3 ribs celery to leaves, diced
    1 piece burdock root, diced
    1 onion, cut into half-moon slices
    1–2 teaspoons olive or other oil to sauté vegetables
    optional: A few sprigs fresh rosemary, chopped
    1/2 bunch flat-leaf parsley, chopped (for garnish)

To cook beans: Pour off soaking water from the beans, place kombu in beans and cover with new water an inch above the beans. Bring to a boil on high heat, cover, reduce heat to low and simmer for 1 hour. After 1 hour, test the beans for tenderness. If still slightly hard, cook 30 minutes longer. Check water level during cooking and add more if needed. Add salt 10 minutes before the end of cooking time (don't salt the beans until they're tender).

While the beans are cooking: Chop the carrot, celery, and burdock. Cut the onion into half-moon slices. Sauté the onion and add a pinch of salt, for 2 minutes in olive oil on medium-high heat. Add the burdock, carrot, and rosemary and sauté for 3 to 4 more minutes. Add the celery and sauté for 3 to 4 more minutes.

Add half of the cooked beans to the vegetable mixture. Puree the other half of the beans with a potato masher on the stovetop in another pan, and then add them to the whole beans and vegetable mixture. Add enough water to make a brothy consistency. Bring the soup to a gentle boil on high heat, reduce to low, cover, and simmer for 10 minutes.

Stir in half the parsley. Garnish each portion of soup with the rest while serving. Enjoy with a delicious whole grain and green leafy vegetable.

Serves 6–8

Best Vegan Chili

Consider serving this chili over cornbread, polenta, or brown rice, with a leafy green or side of other fresh vegetables.

> 2 cups kidney beans, soaked overnight, then drained
> 1-inch piece kombu
> 1/2 teaspoon sea salt
> 1 onion, diced
> 1 teaspoon olive oil
> 1/2 of 10-ounce package organic frozen corn (or fresh)
> *optional:* 1/2 teaspoon chili powder, 1 teaspoon cumin, 1 teaspoon paprika
> 1 cup Pastor Chuck's brand medium apple salsa (or your favorite salsa)
> 1 cup chopped seitan
> 1 tablespoon tamari soy sauce
> 1/4 cup fresh chopped parsley for garnish

Put the beans in a soup pot with enough fresh spring or filtered water to cover. Add the kombu to the pot. Bring to a boil on high heat, cover, reduce heat to low, and simmer for 1 hour.

After an hour, check the beans for tenderness. If not tender, cook for 15 more minutes, or more as needed. If tender, add sea salt and cook for 10 more minutes.

While beans are cooking, sauté the onion in olive oil in a skillet over medium-high heat until translucent. Add the corn and stir until heated. Add spices if desired and cook for 3 to 4 minutes while stirring.

When the beans are done, add the onion mixture to the beans, along with the salsa, chopped seitan, and soy sauce. Cook for 5 to 10 more minutes. Add parsley to garnish.

Serve warm over cornbread, polenta, or brown rice with a side of fresh vegetables.

Serves 6

Cannellini Bean Soup

2 cups dried cannellini beans, washed and soaked overnight

1/4 teaspoon sea salt

2 carrots, chopped

3 ribs celery, chopped

1 onion, chopped

fresh rosemary, chopped

1/2 cup fresh parsley, chopped

optional: dried spices such as oregano and basil

Put the beans in a large soup pot and add water to cover. Bring to a boil over high heat, cover, reduce heat to low, and simmer for 60 to 90 minutes, or until beans are soft.

Add sea salt and cook for 10 more minutes. Remove half the beans and puree them in a food processor, then add them back to the soup pot.

Add vegetables and optional spices, plus additional water to make the soup as brothy as you like. Simmer for 20 more minutes. Garnish with parsley.

Serves 6–8

Basic Miso Soup

1/2- to 1-inch piece wakame sea vegetable (available at most health-food stores) per cup of soup

2 1/2 cups water

1/2 to 1 cup finely sliced vegetable (such as carrot, daikon radish, onion, broccoli, cauliflower, cabbage, leek, shiitake mushroom. Use one or more vegetables)

3/4 to 1 teaspoon miso paste per cup of soup (2 for this recipe)

1 teaspoon finely chopped scallion garnish per cup of soup

Place the wakame in a small cup of water to soak until it is tender (5 minutes). Finely slice the wakame and place it in a sauce pan with fresh spring or filtered tap water. Bring to a boil, uncovered, over medium heat.

When the water is boiling, add the finely sliced vegetables. Simmer until they are tender, about 3 to 5 minutes. In a mug or small bowl, add the miso paste to a small amount of water and stir until blended. Pour the diluted miso into the lightly simmering broth and cook for 5 more minutes. Serve garnished with chopped scallion.

Serves 2

Barley Mushroom Soup

3 cups whole barley (soaked overnight and covered with water)

1 teaspoon light sesame oil

1 onion, sliced thinly into half-moons

5 or 6 cups mushroom stock (I usually use only water, but another option is 1 cube
  of bouillon (I recommend vegan bouillon. If bouillon is used, omit the soy sauce)

4 or 5 dried shiitake mushrooms, soaked until tender, thinly sliced

1 (8-ounce) package button mushrooms, washed, thinly sliced

1 tablespoon soy sauce ($1/2$ teaspoon sea salt can be substituted)

2 ribs celery, thinly sliced

fresh scallions, thinly sliced for garnish

optional: You also may use pearled barley, a cracked form of the whole grain

Rinse barley well by placing it in a pot and covering with water. Rub gently between the palms of your hands and drain. Then refill the pot for soaking. After soaking the barley overnight, drain and discard the soaking water.

In a soup pot, heat oil and sauté the onions until they are translucent. Add stock and barley and bring to a boil over high heat. Stir in the mushrooms, reduce heat to low and cook, covered, for 45 to 60 minutes until barley becomes soft and creamy. Add more water as needed for soup consistency.

Season lightly with soy sauce or salt. Simmer for 10 to 15 minutes more. Stir in the raw celery for some crunch. Garnish with fresh scallions and serve.

Serves 6–8

Exotic Stew

I like this stew's somewhat exotic ingredients: dried lotus root, dried tofu, and dried daikon, mixed with black soybeans and veggies. Eating soup before a meal is a good way to relax your digestive system and prepare it for the rest of the meal. I might have with this soup: a small portion of brown rice, a medley of vegetables (Brussels sprouts, carrots, and cauliflower, maybe), some steamed greens, leftover pressed salad.

1 cup black soybeans (soak overnight, covered with water)

2-inch strip kombu, rinsed

1 stalk celery, diced

1 onion, diced

1 cup butternut squash, cubed

$1/2$ cup fresh or dried lotus root, sliced, reconstituted in a cup of water for 10 minutes

$1/2$ cup minced burdock

1 cup dried daikon, soaked for 10 minutes (discard soaking water)

5 pieces dried tofu soaked to reconstitute, rinsed, and sliced (fresh tofu can be used)

$1/2$ teaspoon sea salt

1 tablespoon soy sauce

1 tablespoon barley malt

parsley or cilantro as a garnish

Place the kombu on the bottom of a pot and add the black soybeans with their soaking water. Make sure the water is high enough to cover the beans by 1 inch. Add more water if needed. Bring beans to a boil over medium-high heat, cover, reduce heat to low and simmer for 1 hour.

Add the celery, onion, squash, lotus root, burdock, dried daikon, and tofu. Add more water to make a stew-like consistency; start with 6 cups.

Bring the pot back to a boil over high heat, cover, reduce heat to low, and cook for 30 more minutes. Add sea salt and cook for 5 to 10 more minutes. Add soy sauce and barley malt and cook for another 5 to 7 minutes.

Serve hot, garnished with minced parsley or cilantro.

Serves 6–8

George's Tuscan Bean and Bread Hearty Stew

In January 1999, Dr. Devra Krassner, a naturopath, told me that "some women with breast cancer have been helped by the macrobiotic (a plant-based) diet." She later told me that her father George Krassner had adopted this way of eating when he was diagnosed in 1988 with advanced prostate cancer, which was expected to be terminal. My husband and I met George and his wife Judith on a trip to Italy in 2001. After that, we got together each year when they came up from Chapel Hill, North Carolina, to Maine to visit their children. When I saw George in summer 2009, he was 80. He continues to live a healthy and active life, continues to travel, and still beats his 20-year-old grandson at tennis (almost).

1 1/2 cups pre-soaked cannellini beans
1/4 cup olive oil
2 small ribs celery
1 cup chopped yellow onion
2 carrots, sliced in rounds
2 cups green cabbage, coarsely chopped
16-ounce can stewed tomatoes
2 cups coarsely chopped kale
sea salt, black pepper, garlic, shoyu to taste
3 slices sourdough or whole-grain bread, cut into bite-size pieces

Soak beans overnight. Bring the beans to a boil on high heat. Cover, reduce heat to low, and cook for 1 hour or until tender.

Optional: Set aside 3/4 cup cooked beans; puree the remaining beans with the cooking liquid.

Heat olive oil on low to medium heat in a soup pan, then add the celery, onion, carrots, and cabbage. Stir well and sauté for 3 to 5 minutes. Add tomatoes and water to cover. Simmer for 20 minutes.

Add the beans (and the puree, if used). Simmer covered for 1/2 hour. Add chopped kale and cook for 8 more minutes. Season with spices to taste. Stir in bread and serve.

Serves 6

George says: "I'm pleased to credit my friend, Ginger Seles, a holistic chef, caterer and purveyor of natural skin-care products, for the basis of this recipe."

Bart's Long-Life Soup

I met Bart Potenza, owner of two hugely popular vegan restaurants (Candle 79 and The Candle Café in New York City), a couple of years ago via Kathy and Tom Freston, who were hosting a Physicians Committee for Responsible Medicine event at their home. Later that evening, as fate would have it, we had a reservation to eat at Candle 79, so we were able to taste some of Bart's heavenly food—and boy, what a treat! I later learned that Bart started The Candle Café after winning the lottery. I love it when good things happen to good people.

$^1/_2$ cup dried shiitake mushrooms

$^1/_2$ cup arame

1 tablespoon olive oil

1 yellow onion, peeled, halved, and thinly sliced

$^1/_4$ cup minced garlic

$^1/_2$ cup peeled and minced ginger

$^1/_2$ cup shoyu or tamari (wheat free)

$^1/_2$ to 1 teaspoon cayenne

2 teaspoons brown rice vinegar

2 teaspoons sesame oil

13 $^1/_2$ cups water

Place the shiitake mushrooms and the arame in two separate bowls and pour 4 $^1/_2$ cups of hot water over each. Let the bowls sit for 15 minutes each.

Drain the mushrooms, but save the water. Thinly slice the mushrooms. Drain and rinse the arame and discard the water. Coarsely chop the arame. Heat the olive oil in a sauté pan on medium heat and cook the onion, garlic, and ginger until softened, about 10 minutes. Transfer to a soup pot and add the shoyu, cayenne (according to taste), vinegar, and sesame oil. Add the reserved mushroom water, mushrooms, and arame.

Add an additional 4 $^1/_2$ cups of water to the pot, bring to a boil on high, reduce heat to low, and simmer, uncovered, for 10 minutes. Serve immediately.

Serves 6–8

Bart says: "Chef Chris Fox introduced this appropriately named soup to the Candle. Ginger, garlic, and cayenne pepper are loaded with health benefits. They are said to increase circulation and stimulate metabolisms, as well as build up immune systems. Whether you're feeling a cold coming on or not, this is an excellent soup to eat for your health and well-being."

Hold-the-Chicken Chicken Soup

    3 cups red lentils
    8 cups water
    1 or 2 teaspoons olive (or sesame) oil
    1 onion, diced
    $^1/_2$ to 1 teaspoon sea salt
    3 ribs of celery, diced
    2 two large carrots, diced
    10 white button mushrooms, quartered
    $^1/_2$ cup dried maitake mushrooms, soaked in water for 30 minutes to reconstitute
    1 pound tofu (I used organic Soy Boy brand), cut into cubes
    2 cups organic penne pasta (I use seminola, but rice pasta can be substituted)
    $^1/_2$ cup fresh parsley, chopped
    optional: 1 teaspoon of "The Blend," a combination of dried parsley, basil, marjoram,
        chervil, garlic, and spices from The Maine Accent in Hallowell, Maine

Pour the red lentils into a bowl with water and wash them by rubbing between your hands. This will release the saponins—a bitter-tasting, natural coating that I've heard works as a natural insect repellent.

Drain the lentils and add to a soup pot with 8 cups of water. Bring to a boil on high heat, reduce heat to low, and simmer, covered, for 30 minutes. In a separate skillet (I use cast iron), sauté the onion in olive or sesame oil on medium-high heat.

Add sea salt and optional herbs and sauté for 1 to 2 minutes. Add the celery and carrot and sauté for 2 more minutes. Add the white button mushrooms and sauté for 2 to 3 more minutes. Add the sautéed vegetables and the maitakes to the soup pot with the lentils.

Return to a boil on high heat, then reduce heat to medium-low and keep simmering. Add the tofu cubes and the pasta. Return to a boil, then reduce heat to simmer, and continue cooking for 10 more minutes.

Garnish with fresh parsley. Serve with steamed greens or other vegetables as a meal. Serves 6–8

sea vegetables

Gems from the Sea

Have you ever eaten sea vegetables, a.k.a. seaweed? If you like sushi, you've no doubt eaten nori, the sea plant in which sushi is typically wrapped.

Sea vegetables are among the most beneficial foods you can eat. According to George Mateljan's The World's Healthiest Foods, "Sea vegetables are an excellent source of iodine and vitamin K; a very good source of the B-vitamin folate, and magnesium; and a good source of iron, calcium, and the B-vitamins riboflavin and pantothenic acid. In addition, sea vegetables contain good amounts of lignans, plant compounds with cancer-protective properties." Arame, for example, is a mineral-rich brown algae. Many people who try it for the first time are surprised by its mild, sweet flavor.

Another sea vegetable, wakame, is commonly used in miso soup and also cooked in beans to help aid in digestion. Only a postage-stamp-size piece is needed. It's typically taken from a package in its dried form and reconstituted for a few minutes in water, then added to the soup or other dish in which it's being used.

Kombu is used the same way. I usually add a 1-inch piece of it to beans that I'm cooking, to add minerals and to make the beans more easily digestible.

To store unused sea vegetables, I either keep them in a resealable plastic bag or put them in a glass jar with a lid (the same way I store my grains). They keep for a very long time. I'm guessing they would keep for years, but you'll probably (hopefully) eat them long before then.

I'm often asked how much seaweed is appropriate in a diet. I use very small amounts when cooking with kombu and wakame. The general rule with seaweed is more is not better, as a little adds a lot of minerals. The exception is arame—I have about a quarter cup for a serving.

Sea vegetables are believed to have cancer-healing properties, too. If all of that is not enough to convince you, look at some of these appetizing, easy starter dishes. Expand your horizons. You might be surprised.

Arame Carrot Sauté

I try to make this dish every other week.

1/2 of a 1.75-ounce package arame
1 teaspoon sesame oil
1 carrot, grated
1/2 cup water
1 teaspoon soy sauce
2 scallions, thinly sliced
1/2 cup water
1 tablespoon mirin (I use Eden brand)

Soak dried arame in water for 5 to 10 minutes to reconstitute, then discard the soaking water. Heat sesame oil on medium heat in a cast-iron skillet. Add the arame and sauté, stirring occasionally, for 5 minutes.

Add the carrot and water and turn heat to high until the mixture is boiling. Reduce heat to low and simmer for 20 minutes. Add mirin and soy sauce and cook for 5 more minutes. Place in a serving dish and garnish with scallions.

Serves 10–12 (1/4- to 1/3-cup portions)

Note: This recipe may also be refrigerated, then eaten over a three-day period.

Arame-Stuffed Mushrooms

Sandy Pukel is such a friendly, outgoing guy that his success is no surprise. I first met him in person at a Kushi Institute conference in Boston in 2007. He owned and ran a health food store in Miami for many years, then started a healthy-cruise business. The Taste of Health Cruise has been a huge success, serving vegan meals and offering lectures and classes by many well-known experts in the field of wellness. It was listed in National Geographic's The 100 Best Worldwide Vacations to Enrich Your Life. Sandy has written a book along with chef Mark Hanna featuring many of the recipes served on the cruise over the past several years, Grains and Greens on the Deep Blue Sea. This is one of their great recipes.

2 cups arame (half a 1.75-ounce package)
$1/2$ cup water
optional: 1 tablespoon sake
2 tablespoon shoyu
1 tablespoon sesame oil
$1/2$ cup onion, finely chopped
1 tablespoon fresh ginger juice
1 cup walnut halves, lightly toasted
20 large button mushrooms (about 2-inches in diameter), stems removed
$1/2$ cup parsley, chopped
1 lemon, cut into wedges

Preheat oven to 350 degrees.

Rinse the arame and place in a medium bowl. Add enough water to cover and let it soak for 10 minutes, or until reconstituted. Drain the arame and discard the water.

Place the arame in a medium saucepan with the water, sake (if using), and shoyu. Bring to a boil on high heat, then reduce heat to medium-low and simmer uncovered for 10 minutes, or until the liquid has cooked away. Remove the arame from the pan with a slotted spoon and place in a food processor or blender.

In a small skillet, heat sesame oil over medium-low heat, then add the onions. Sauté for 5 minutes or until the onions are translucent. Add ginger juice and stir well. Add the sautéed onion and walnut halves to the food processor with the arame. Blend well, but do not make completely smooth.

Fill each mushroom cap with arame mixture, packing firmly and mounding it until all the mixture is used. Arrange caps in an oiled baking dish.

Cover pan lightly with aluminum foil. Bake at 350 degrees for 20 minutes, or until the mushrooms are cooked. Serve hot, garnished with parsley and lemon wedges.

Serves 4–6

Variations:
- Use hijiki instead of arame.
- Substitute mirin for sake.
- Decrease nuts to $^1\!/_2$ cup and add $^1\!/_2$ cup pitted black olives.
- Use arame mixture as a paté or sandwich spread.
- Instead of button mushrooms, stuff 3 or 4 portabella mushrooms.
- To serve, cut into wedges with a sharp knife.

Emerald Arame Sauté

1 (1.75-ounce) package arame
1 teaspoon sesame oil
$^1\!/_2$ cup or more of the soaking water
20 fresh green beans, washed, sliced into $^1\!/_4$-inch pieces
optional: 2 teaspoons mirin (I use Eden brand)
2 teaspoons soy sauce
1 cup fresh cilantro, washed, stems mostly removed, chopped

Cover arame in water (about 16 ounces) and soak to reconstitute for 5 to 10 minutes (longer if desired). Drain, but save the soaking water.

Heat the sesame oil on medium-high heat in a cast-iron skillet. Add the arame and sauté, stirring occasionally, for 5 minutes. Reduce heat as the pan heats up. (Stir-frying in oil helps the minerals to be more easily absorbed by the body, which is also good for the bones.)

Add $^1\!/_2$ cup of the soaking water, turn heat to high, and bring to a boil. Reduce heat to low and simmer for 5 more minutes. Add green beans, mirin, and soy sauce. Cover and cook for 5 more minutes. Immediately place in a serving dish, let cool for 5 to 10 minutes, and garnish with cilantro.

Serves about 20 ($^1\!/_8$- to $^1\!/_4$-cup portions)

Note: This dish can be eaten over a three-day period if refrigerated.

Wakame Bakeame

2 cups wakame, washed, reconstituted, and sliced
3 to 5 tablespoons tahini (paste of sesame seeds and olive oil)
1 to 1 1/2 cups water
1 teaspoon tamari (soy sauce)
1/2 teaspoon ginger juice
1 to 2 cups onion, chopped
3/4 cup corn, cut fresh from cob or frozen
1/4 cup sesame seeds

Preheat oven to 375 degrees.

Puree the tahini, water, and tamari, add ginger juice. Mix in the onions, corn, and wakame.

Place in a casserole dish, sprinkle with sesame seeds. Cover and bake for 30 to 35 minutes. Uncover and bake for 10 more minutes. You may need to add a small amount of water during baking if it gets too dry.

Serves 3–4

Lemony Sesame Arame

1 (2.1-ounce) package arame
1 tablespoon soy sauce
1 teaspoon grated lemon rind
1/2 cup ground roasted sesame seeds
scallions, sliced for garnish

Rinse the arame in a strainer under running water. Place in a pot with enough water to cover and let sit for 3 to 5 minutes. Bring to a boil on high heat, cover, reduce heat to medium-low, and simmer for 10 minutes. Remove the lid, add soy sauce, and boil until all the liquid has evaporated.

Add the lemon rind and sesame seeds and mix well. Garnish with fresh sliced scallions and serve with lemon wedges.

Serves 10–12

Happy Hijiki

Hijiki is a brown sea vegetable that grows wild around Japan, China, and Korea.

1 cup hijiki

3 cups water

1 medium onion, sliced

1 carrot, sliced into matchsticks

1 tablespoon toasted sesame oil

4 sliced shiitake mushrooms (if using dried, soak for 10 minutes, remove stems,
 use water)

1 cup apple juice (or $1/2$ cup juice and $1/2$ cup water)

2 tablespoons tamari soy sauce

1 teaspoon fresh grated ginger juice

parsley to garnish

Soak the hijiki for 10 minutes in water. Strain and keep the soaking water. Sauté the onions and carrots in sesame oil on medium heat until onions are transparent, about 5 minutes.

Add the hijiki, shiitake, and soaking water, plus apple juice to cover surface. Turn heat to high and bring to a boil, then cover and simmer for 40 minutes to evaporate most of the liquid.

Garnish with parsley and serve hot as a side dish or chilled over a bed of lettuce.

Serves 6

Sweet Potato and Arame Salad with Asian-Style Tartar Sauce

Aine McAteer of Ireland puts a new spin on arame with this salad. I first met Aine through her blog on Oprah.com, and then read her story about how she healed her thyroid disease by following a plant-based diet. When she friended me on Facebook, I happily accepted and went on to read these fabulous recipes she is creating while visiting her parents in Ireland, after foraging for nettles, mushrooms, and other wild foods. Aine writes for The Independent, *one of Ireland's leading magazines. Her delectable sea vegetable salad will brighten any day!*

2 large sweet potatoes
2 parsnips
2 tablespoons olive oil
pinch of sea salt
black pepper
1 cup dry arame, reconstituted
1 tablespoon tamari
1 tablespoon mirin
1 teaspoon toasted sesame oil
salad greens, such as arugula or watercress, to serve
toasted sesame seeds

Tartar Sauce
1/2 cup mayonnaise or vegan mayonnaise
1 tablespoon minced pickled ginger
1 tablespoon wasabi paste
1 small shallot, finely minced
1 teaspoon umeboshi plum vinegar
2 tablespoons minced cilantro
big squeeze of lime juice

Preheat oven to 375 degrees.

Peel the sweet potato and parsnips and cut into bite-size chunks. Steam the chunks for about 5 minutes, until they just start to soften up (you can do this in a steamer basket set over boiling water or by simmering in a small amount of water).

In the meantime, pour the olive oil onto a baking tray and let it heat up in the oven. Transfer the potato and parsnip chunks to the oven-warmed tray and sprinkle with salt and black pepper. Toss to coat the vegetables evenly with the oil. Put on top shelf of oven and bake for about 20 minutes, until they're tender when pricked with a fork.

While the veggies are baking, prepare the arame and tartar sauce. Measure out the arame dry, then soak in a bowl with enough water to cover for 10 to 15 minutes. Drain and simmer the arame in about ¼ cup of the soaking water—drizzle with the tamari and mirin while cooking. After about 10 minutes, turn the heat up a bit to cook off any excess liquid and drizzle with the toasted sesame oil. Mix together all the tartar sauce ingredients.

To serve, arrange the salad greens on plates or a serving platter, and top with the arame and sweet potato mixture. Add a big dollop of the tartar sauce and sprinkle some toasted sesame seeds on top.

Variations: You can use other veggies, such as sweet squash or pumpkin, in place of the sweet potato. You could also add corn, zucchini, or other vegetables.

If you don't like the tartar sauce too spicy, omit the wasabi. Instead, add other ingredients like minced capers, chives, parsley, or minced dill pickle.

Serves 4–6

Mushrooms with Sea Palm

This side dish is nice on a bed of salad greens, layered with a little brown rice and garnished with a few nuts. Steam a side of delicious leafy kale and voila, a tasty lunch.

> 4 or 5 fresh mushrooms, sliced thinly (any variety)
> 1 small onion
> ½ teaspoon sesame oil
> 1 cup sea palm, cut into small pieces
> ½ cup water
> ½ teaspoon tamari (or 1 teaspoon miso)

Slice the mushrooms and cut the onion in half and slice into half-moons. Add oil to a pan and sauté the mushrooms and onion over medium heat until the onion is translucent.

Add the sea palm and water. Cover and simmer for 20 minutes. Season with tamari.

Serves 4–6

Sea Palm and Corn

I've always liked the light taste of sea palm, the mildest of sea vegetables. Add a little corn and lots of fresh parsley, and you have a light, tasty sea veggie side dish.

1 (4-ounce) package sea palm, soaked to reconstitute, drained, and sliced into
    bite-size pieces (save the soaking water)
2 teaspoons sesame oil
1 cup organic frozen corn (or fresh)
$^1/_2$ cup soaking water
1 or 2 teaspoons shoyu
optional: 1 tablespoon mirin
$^1/_3$ cup parsley, chopped

Place the sea palm in a bowl with water to cover and soak for 20 to 30 minutes to reconstitute. Drain, but save the soaking water.

Heat sesame oil in a cast-iron skillet on medium-high, add sea palm, and stir-fry for 2 to 3 minutes. Add corn and stir-fry for 1 more minute. Add $^1/_2$ cup of the soaking water, shoyu (and optional mirin), and bring to a boil. Reduce heat to medium-low and simmer for 5 to 10 more minutes, or until the water is almost gone.

Add parsley, stir, and enjoy.

Serves 4

Vegetable Stir-Fry with Arame

Sea vegetables typically make great side dishes. This recipe shows that seaweed can be a good complement and add a lot of nutrients to other dishes.

1 onion, cut in half, sliced thinly

$1/8$ teaspoon sea salt

1 tablespoon sesame oil

2 cups green cabbage, sliced thinly

3 small carrots, sliced thinly on a diagonal

3 large dried shiitake mushrooms, reconstituted in 2 cups of water for 20 minutes or
    until soft, cut in half and sliced thinly (save the soaking water)

2 teaspoons soy sauce

optional: 1 tablespoon mirin

1 cup of rapini (broccoli rabe), sliced in pieces

$1/4$ cup arame, soaked 10 minutes and drained

1 tablespoon kuzu, diluted in 1 cup of the mushroom soaking water

2-inch piece of ginger, grate and squeeze the juice

In a skillet on medium-high heat, sauté the onion and salt in dill for 1 minute. Add the cabbage and cook another 1 to 2 minutes. Add the carrot and stir-fry for 2 to 3 more minutes.

Add the shiitake mushrooms and a $1/4$ cup of the soaking water and cook for 5 minutes. Add soy sauce, mirin, rapini, and arame. Cook for 2 more minutes.

Add the diluted kuzu, stir until it thickens and coats vegetables. Add more water to thin if needed for desired consistency. Cook for 1 to 2 more minutes. Turn off heat, add ginger juice, and stir. Serve over brown rice or other grain (or noodles).

Serves 4–6

Even Small Changes
Can Make a Difference

Even small changes in what we choose to eat can make an enormous difference in our health. If you're like most busy people, it can be tough to find time to cook good meals. The key, then, is making conscious, wise choices. My husband Tom has a great suggestion for anyone making improvements in their diet: "Think of it as crowding out some of your less-than-healthy food choices." Little changes encourage more little changes. And these eventually add up to a better way of eating. These are all steps in the right direction:

1. You guessed it . . . add more fresh vegetables! Fresh organic is best, but if you can't get organic, don't let this be a show-stopper.

2. Eat fruit for dessert in place of junk or non-nutritive foods high in sugar and chemical additives. Whole fruits eaten in season are better choices than fruit juices.

3. Add whole grains to your diet once a day. As Americans, we're not used to whole grains other than brown rice. Fortunately, that's a good one to start with!

4. Add beans to your diet—black beans, kidney beans, chickpeas, lentils . . . the list goes on. Learn to cook beans, or start with organic canned beans.

5. Snacks: Nuts (almonds, pecans, walnuts, peanuts), seeds (such as pumpkin and sunflower), and dried fruits are excellent healthy choices.

6. Beverages: Drink filtered tap or spring water; cut down on caffeine.

7. Keep a limited supply or no junk foods in your living area and lots of the good stuff! It's about developing good habits.

8. Try your best to eat three meals a day, with no late-night eating. I know breakfast is a hard one for some folks, but a bowl of oatmeal–even if it's instant–with a small handful of organic trail mix and or seasonal fruit will keep you alert and satiated until lunch.

salads

Strawberry Shiitake Salad

My daughter Cammie is the best eater, and you can tell by looking at her. She's tall, slim, and doesn't struggle with weight or health problems. It wasn't always so. She was 8 when we changed over to a healthy diet—and until then she had allergies to different foods and it affected her behavior. When she ate eggs, she had tantrums. While eating standard American diet foods, both of my kids had frequent runny noses, ear infections, and colds. Getting junk and processed foods out of our cabinets and getting Cammie off eggs, cheese, and other dairy and other animal protein really helped. After switching to whole grains, beans, vegetables, and mostly fruit for snacks, her attention span and grades improved dramatically. She was a competitive downhill skier and soccer player through high school and eating this way helped keep her strong, healthy, and free from colds, the flu, and other ailments her friends got during long and grueling ski and soccer seasons. Now in college, Cammie helps keep me in line by reminding me not to eat too much, or between meals! She has definitely seen the benefit of a plant-based diet and lifestyle. This salad is her creation.

> 1 head romaine, torn into bite-size pieces
> a few handfuls of baby spinach
> 1 pint fresh organic strawberries, sliced thinly
> 10 shiitake mushrooms, sliced thinly
> olive oil, or sunflower oil
> golden balsamic vinegar
> pinch of sea salt or dash of soy sauce

Simply combine torn Romaine, baby spinach, fresh-sliced shiitake mushrooms, and organic strawberries. For an easy dressing, blend together a little extra virgin olive oil and balsamic vinegar. Add a pinch of salt or a dash of soysauce if desired.

Serves 2–4

Bok Choy Pressed Salad

Tasty, low-cal pressed salads are packed with nutrients and enzymes, and are easy to make. They keep well in the refrigerator for a few days, too. The possibilities of vegetable combinations are endless, and there are countless low-cal dressings you can try. (I happen to like mine plain!)

3 small heads baby bok choy
$1/2$ large daikon, cut in matchsticks or grated
1 or 2 carrots, cut in matchsticks or large grated
2 ribs celery, sliced thin
$1/2$ package bean sprouts
$1/2$ teaspoon of sea salt per cup of vegetables

Put all the vegetables, except the bean sprouts, into a large bowl and massage the salt into them. Place a small dish on top of the veggies (to press) and weight with something heavy (such as a jar of rice). Let it press for 15 minutes, until a lot of water is expelled. This helps break down the fiber and make the vegetables more digestible while still keeping the enzymes intact.

Drain off the liquid, then rinse with a few cups of water to wash off the excess salt—it has done its job! This salad should not taste salty. If so, rinse with more water. Add the bean sprouts (for more crunch) and toss.

Asian Cabbage Salad

1 head purple cabbage, sliced thinly (about 6 cups)
1 large carrot, grated
1/4 cup cilantro, chopped

Marinade:

2 tablespoons olive oil
1 teaspoon hot pepper sesame oil
2 tablespoons brown rice syrup
1/2 cup water
1 tablespoon brown rice vinegar
1 tablespoon lemon juice
1/4 teaspoon sea salt
1 tablespoon tamari (wheat-free soy) sauce

Prepare the cabbage, carrot, and cilantro. Mix the marinade ingredients and add to cabbage. Marinate in refrigerator overnight.

Serves 10–12

Tofu Mayonnaise

8 ounces tofu
1/2 cup water
2 teaspoons sesame or olive oil
1 tablespoon lemon juice
1 tablespoon brown rice vinegar
1 tablespoon mellow white miso (or 1/4 teaspoon sea salt)

Slice tofu and steam over high heat for 3 minutes. Blend all ingredients until smooth. This should keep refrigerated for 2 to 3 days. If it separates, just re-blend.

Confetti Carrot Salad

A favorite, easy, sweet salad. Perfect for summer.

4 large carrots, grated
3 ribs celery, sliced thinly
$1/2$ cup organic apple–juice–sweetened cranberries
$1/2$ cup (more if desired) parsley

Dressing
$1/3$ cup mayonnaise or veggie mayonnaise or homemade Tofu Mayonnaise (p. 120)
$1/8$ cup apple juice
2 tablespoons brown rice syrup
1 tablespoon lemon juice

Mix dressing ingredients and mix the vegetables. Pour the dressing onto the vegetables and cranberries. That's all there is to it!

Serves 1–2

Waldorf Salad

$1/4$ cup toasted walnuts
$1/4$ cup raisins
2 cups apples, diced
2 ribs celery, diced
1 grated carrot
2 tablespoons dulse flakes
veggie or Tofu Mayonnaise (p. 120)
1 teaspoon umeboshi vinegar

Put everything in a bowl and mix in a small amount of vegan or Tofu Mayonnaise. Splash in some umeboshi vinegar. Taste and season to your liking.

Serves 4

Boiled Veggie Salad

1 cup thinly sliced Chinese cabbage
$^{1}/_{2}$ cup thinly sliced leek
1 cup broccoli florets
$^{1}/_{4}$ cup summer squash, sliced into half-rounds
5 or 6 red radishes, halved

Fill a pot half full with spring water. Bring to a rolling boil over medium to high heat. Place each vegetable, one at a time, in the water. Boil uncovered only until the color of the vegetables turns bright—a minute or less.

Blanch each vegetable separately and in order from mildest- to strongest-tasting so that each retains its own distinct flavor and color. Use a fine-mesh skimmer to remove vegetables from boiling water.

Drain each vegetable on a flat surface to stop cooking. Serve plain, with a simple dressing, or a with a splash of vinegar or lemon juice. Serve warm, at room temperature, or chilled, tossed together or arranged in sections on a platter.

Serves 4

Note: Try this with other combinations—whatever you like!

Pickled Purple Onions and Golden Beets

If you have a problem eating raw onions like I do, you'll love knowing that pickling breaks down the fiber and pulls the water out, making them easier to digest.

1 large purple onion, sliced into half moons
3 golden beets, cut in half, sliced thinly into bite-size pieces, and cooked
1/2 teaspoon sea salt
2 fresh lemons, juiced
optional: 1/2 cup chopped fresh parsley or cilantro

To cook beets: Wash, slice, and cover with water. Turn heat to high and bring to a boil. Cover, reduce heat to low, and simmer for 20 minutes. Drain and cool beets.

To assemble ingredients: Place sliced onions and beets in a bowl and sprinkle with sea salt and lemon juice. Mix with a wooden spoon or clean hands. Let stand, covered, in the refrigerator for 6 to 8 hours, stirring two or three times during that period to make sure the lemon juice and salt coats all the vegetables. When ready to serve, drain off juice and garnish with parsley or cilantro if desired.

Serves 4–6

Summer Salad Wrap with Garden Greens and Balsamic Vinaigrette

I met Verne Verona in 2000 at the first Kushi Institute Macrobiotic Conference I attended, in Westfield, Massachusetts. I immediately liked him because he's funny and intelligent, but doesn't take himself too seriously. I noticed that he really connects with people. For example, when he spoke with one of my heroes, Aveline Kushi—who was in a wheelchair at the time—he made a point of crouching down to talk to her at her eye level. He's kind to people, accepting of where they are, and this has inspired me to do the same. Verne's a good writer, too. I enjoyed his Nature's Cancer Fighting Foods *and* Macrobiotics for Dummies, *and he's finishing a book on sexual health. He also takes great photographs and is directing a film.*

Wraps are a fabulous and quick way to create a tasty lunch. While Verne's recipe uses salad ingredients, you can also make wraps with leftovers, rice and beans, tofu and veggies–the list is endless! Feel free to add other ingredients to the salad.

    1 organic tortilla wrap
    1 tablespoon hummus
    $1/_2$ avocado
    1 small carrot, grated
    $1/_4$ cup cucumber, cut into julienne pieces
    1 tablespoon fresh cilantro, chopped
    1 tablespoon mint, chopped
    juice of $1/_4$ lemon
    handful of garden greens

Balsamic Vinaigrette

    2 or 3 tablespoons balsamic vinegar
    $1/_4$ cup extra virgin olive oil
    pinch of sea salt
    1 clove fresh garlic, pressed
    1 tablespoon finely chopped fresh basil

In a small bowl, mix the dressing ingredients, beating them a little until all the ingredients are blended.

Cut the avocado into thin slices. Grate the carrot into a bowl and squeeze lemon juice over it.

Lightly warm the tortilla in a broiler or toaster oven, being careful not to overcook it or it will be too crispy to wrap (2 to 3 minutes is usually fine).

Spread a thin layer of hummus over the whole wrap.

Place the avocado, cucumber, grated carrot, cilantro, and mint in the middle of the tortilla. Sprinkle a pinch of sea salt. Drizzle on some vinaigrette.

Fold in the bottom and top of the wrap until they overlap. Fold in one side to overlap, then the remaining side. This should seal the wrap.

Serves 1

Yam and Pickled-Onion Salad

So fresh and delish!

1 raw red onion, sliced into half moons
1 lemon, juiced
$1/4$ teaspoon sea salt
3 large yams
1 tablespoon balsamic vinegar
1 tablespoon shoyu
2 teaspoons olive oil
1 tablespoon rice syrup
1 cup celery, diced
$1/2$ cup parsley, chopped
$1/3$ cup toasted almonds, sliced
optional: To make this wheat- and gluten-free, use tamari wheat-free soy sauce in place of shoyu soy sauce.

The day before you want to serve this dish, slice the red onion into half-moons. Add lemon juice and salt to the onions. Cover and refrigerate overnight

The next day, wash the yams, use a fork to make some holes in them, and bake for 45 minutes in a pre-heated 350-degree oven. Cool and chop into bite-sized pieces.

Add balsamic vinegar, shoyu, olive oil, rice syrup, celery, and parsley to the pickled-onion mixture. Stir and pour mixture into a bowl with the yams. Mix.

Toast almonds in a dry cast-iron skillet on medium-high heat for 5 minutes, stirring occasionally. Cool and slice. Garnish the salad with almonds.

Serves 10–12

Salade de Fenouil à l'orange

I met Laetitia Cerou through my son Francis. She's from France and had been working in the United States until she got ill with digestive problems from taking a strong round of antibiotics. When all else failed, she adopted a diet based mostly on raw organic plant foods and she has steadily regained her glowing health. Her salads, prepared with loving care and attention to detail, are the best!

2 fennel bulbs
1 tablespoon freshly squeezed lemon juice
1 orange or tangerine
6 tablespoons cold-pressed extra virgin olive oil
2 tablespoons freshly squeezed orange juice
optional: 1/2 tablespoon rice syrup or honey
fleur de sel (or regular sea salt), to taste
freshly ground pepper, to taste
dill, to taste
optional: 5 mint leaves

Remove the stalks from the top of the fennel bulbs. Cut the head in half through the core. Trim out the woody core, then slice the remaining bulb as thinly as possible, using a mandoline if you have one. Add to a bowl and toss with lemon juice to coat.

Grate the zest of the skin of half the orange, being careful to avoid scrapping the bitter white flesh underneath, and add the zest to the bowl.

Slice off the top and bottom of the orange to stabilize it on the cutting board and cut all around it to expose the juicy flesh. Directly over a separate bowl, cut along each side of the membranes of the orange to collect the segments. Squeeze out the remaining juice. Add the segments to the fennel.

In a separate bowl, whisk the olive oil with the freshly squeezed orange juice and the optional honey or rice syrup to make a dressing. Add to the fennel, with a sprinkle or two of the fleur de sel and freshly ground pepper, and toss to coat.

Sprinkle with some fresh dill and the optional mint leaves, preferably minced with scissors.

Serves 4

Caesar Salad

Dressing

> 1 cup almonds
> 2 tablespoons nutritional yeast
> $1/4$ cup olive oil
> 1 tablespoon sesame oil
> juice of 1 lemon
> 2 cloves garlic, minced
> 2 tablespoons tamari wheat–free soy sauce (or $1/2$ teaspoon sea salt)
> $1/4$ cup water

Blend almonds alone in a food processor. Add the garlic and other ingredients, but add the water last, a little at a time, to get the desired consistency.

Add dressing and Homemade Croutons (p. 92) to a large head of ripped romaine.

Snacking Strategies

Like everyone else, I sometimes find myself snacking for reasons other than being hungry—out of boredom or habit. I eat three healthy, balanced meals a day and I don't generally need more than that to keep me satisfied. But occasionally, my husband Tom—who can easily afford extra calories because he exercises hard daily—snacks on some good-quality tortilla chips, and I might be tempted to eat a few. I just try to limit that, but sometimes I'll have homemade popcorn, leftover veggies (during the day), a small handful of almonds or pumpkin seeds, some rice crackers, or a fresh McIntosh apple cut up and sprinkled with cinnamon.

Treats really are treats to me, and I generally save them for special occasions.

How often do I eat dessert? Maybe once a week, if that. I was a junk-food junkie twelve years ago and all I wanted to eat was sugar. I gave up white sugar, brown sugar, high fructose corn syrup, and even cane sugar. I got rid of most of the processed sugary foods from my cabinets. Eating three balanced meals a day—including *lots* of vegetables—really helps me keep from craving sweets. If I skipped meals, as I did in the past, I'm sure I'd be craving something, but I *never* skip a meal! Seriously. I have a big appetite. If I make a dessert, now, it's a healthy homemade one, sweetened with fruit, fruit juice, brown rice syrup, or, on a special occasion, maple syrup (or a combination of brown rice and maple syrups).

I know I'm kind of a girl scout about sweets and treats, but I have to be. I had cancer twice and I've suffered enough for one lifetime with bad eating habits!

That said, judge for yourself what's best for you. If you crave something deliciously healthy, make one of the following recipes! Just enjoy in *moderation*.

snacks & desserts

Slam-Dunk Guacamole

I saw John Salley on the Rachael Ray Show *and was happy to see this outstanding ath-lete promoting a vegan way of eating! I love that he cooks, too, and when his daughters help him, they have to stand on a stool, just like Rachael did. (The retired three-time NBA champion is 6-foot-11!) John is also an actor and talk show host.*

    1 cup frozen corn kernels, thawed in boiling water for 5 minutes and drained
    2 jalapeño peppers, stemmed, seeded, and chopped
    1/4 medium red onion, chopped
    1 tablespoon virgin organic olive oil
    1 tablespoon virgin organic coconut oil
    2 ripe avocados, peeled and seeded
    4 tablespoons fresh lime juice
    1/4 cup cilantro, chopped
    1 mango, chopped
    1/2 cup Thai Green Curry Sauce (Trader Joe's)
    1 tablespoon Celtic Sea Salt (or regular sea salt)

In a large mixing bowl, toss the corn, jalapeños, onion, olive oil, and coconut oil, then sauté in a pan over medium heat until lightly browned.

In a large mixing bowl, coarsely mash the avocados with lime juice. Stir in the sautéed vegetables, cilantro, chopped mango, Thai Green Curry sauce, salt, and serve.

Serves 2–4

Note: You may want to double or even triple this recipe, especially for larger groups.

Decadent Popcorn

This recipe is adapted from one from my friend and fellow macrobiotic counselor John Kozinski. I use plain organic popping corn and a bit of organic vegetable oil for popping.

   10 cups popped corn
   salt to taste
   ³/₄ cup of rice or barley malt syrup (pure unsweetened maple syrup may be
      substituted, too)
   1 cup roasted peanuts (other additions may include your favorite kind of nuts or
      dried fruits)

Preheat oven to 300 degrees.

   Mix the popcorn and peanuts in a large bowl. Heat the syrup with salt in a double boiler or heavy saucepan until it begins to foam. Remove from heat carefully. Pour the syrup over the popcorn mixture and mix well with two large spoons.

   Oil two baking sheets and spread popcorn onto sheets.

   Bake for 10 minutes or until the candy popcorn is no longer sticky to the touch. Spread on sheets of waxed paper to dry.

Toasted Pumpkin Seeds

Scoop straight from the pumpkin or buy the seeds. They make a great healthy snack.

   1 to 2 cups raw organic pumpkin seeds

Put the seeds in a cast-iron skillet on high heat and stir with a wooden spatula or spoon for 1 to 2 minutes. Reduce heat to medium, or even to low, as the pan heats up, to prevent burning. Continue to toast until the seeds are slightly brown, but not burnt or popping. Toasted pumpkin seeds taste delicious on cooked whole grains such as rice or millet, or as a snack. They can also be lightly salted while cooking, if desired.

Portable Rice Balls

When traveling, I always take rice balls with me—along with steamed veggies in plastic bags. Have rice balls, will travel, and they do travel well.

1 sheet toasted nori (sheets of dried seaweed that come in squares, same as veggie sushi is rolled in)

2 cups cooked brown rice (p. 19)

1/2 umeboshi plum (a Japanese pickled plum) for each rice ball

Moisten hands slightly with water. Holding a full sheet of nori in one palm, place about 1/2 cup of cooked brown rice in the center.

Push half an umeboshi plum into the middle of the rice.

Re-moisten hands and wrap nori around the rice. The wetness of your hands will make the nori sheet soft and pliable, easy to form into a ball around the rice. I prefer to make them the size of a small hamburger patty so they are easier to hold while eating. Some people make them ball shaped or in fancy triangles.

Make sure all the rice is covered with nori to keep it from drying out.

Well-made rice balls will last refrigerated up to 3 days.

Super-Bowl Super Dip

2 cans refried beans (I use Amy's brand Organic Refried Black Beans)
1 teaspoon chili powder
1 teaspoon cumin
1 cup water
1 cup soy cheese
1 avocado, peeled and chopped
Juice of 1 lime
1 cup Zukay's Live Salsa (or other salsa)
$1/2$ cup tofu sour cream (try Tofutti brand or make your own)
1 handful black or green olives, pitted and sliced
2 green onions, chopped
salad greens or shredded Napa cabbage

Heat the refried beans, chili powder, and cumin in a pan on high. Add water, stir, and heat for 2 to 3 minutes. Reduce heat to low and stir until the mixture becomes bubbly, or a consistency that is easily dip-able.

Spread salad greens or Napa cabbage on a serving dish. When the beans are warmed, spread them out on the greens.

Quickly spread the soy cheese on top so that it can melt a little.

Toss the avocados in the lime juice and layer them on next.

Layer on the Zukay's Live Salsa, sour cream, black olives, and green onions.

Serve with tortilla chips and/or veggie sticks. I like Garden of Eaten' Organic Blue Corn Chips—just don't eat the whole bag!

Tofu Sour Cream

Bring one pound of tofu (1 package) to a boil in 2 inches of water and boil for 5 minutes. Drain water, then add a washed and chopped bunch of cilantro (or parsley if desired). Blend in a food processor with the juice of half a lemon or lime.

Lemony Hummus

This hummus is wonderful on carrots, cucumbers, whole-grain bread, whole-wheat pita bread, practically anything. And it's so easy to whip together.

4 or 5 cups cooked chickpeas, or canned
1/4 cup extra virgin olive oil
1/4 cup sesame tahini
optional: 1 clove garlic, crushed
juice of 2 good-size lemons
3/4 cup water
1/8 teaspoon sea salt
optional: few dashes of paprika

Soak chickpeas in water overnight, drain soaking water, rinse. You can also boil them for a few minutes to make sure they're not crunchy.

Combine ingredients in a food processor until smooth, scraping sides a few times as you go.

Serves 2–4

Applesauce for One

1 crisp red (organic if possible) apple, diced (keep skin on, it will soften)
pinch of sea salt
$^{1}/_{2}$ cup water
optional: sprinkle of cinnamon to garnish

Add water, apple, and salt to a small saucepan. Heat to a boil, cover, reduce heat to low, and simmer for 15 minutes. Mash with a fork or potato masher. Put into a dish and sprinkle with a tiny amount of cinnamon (but don't mask the flavor of the apple). Eat warm or chill.

Can't-Resist Kanten

Try this with other kinds of fruit, too.

3 cups organic apple juice (I like Bionature brand)
1 cup water
4 generous tablespoons of kanten flakes (a gelatin-like substance derived from
   red algae—the dried flakes can be found in most health-food stores)
pinch of sea salt
1 cup organic cherries, cut and pitted
sprigs of mint

Bring apple juice and water to a boil, then reduce heat to low and add the kanten flakes and salt. Increase heat to medium-high and simmer for 5 to 10 minutes, stirring occasionally until the flakes are dissolved.

Stir in the cherries. Pour into separate serving-size dishes and let sit for a few hours until jelled. Garnish with mint leaves.

Serves 4–6

Poached Pears with Ginger Almond Cream

Make this special dessert for your honey on Valentine's Day. It's elegant and amazing.

> 4 pears
> 2- to 3-inch cinnamon sticks
> 1 ¹/₂ cups 100 percent pear juice
> ¹/₂ teaspoon nutmeg
> ¹/₂ teaspoon cardamom

Peel the pears and square off the bottoms for standing in pot. Put cinnamon sticks in between the pears. Pour pear juice over all. Sprinkle nutmeg and cardamom into the juice. Bring to a slow boil over medium heat, simmer for 35 minutes. Take the pears out. Continue cooking to reduce syrup, then drizzle over the pears.

Almond Cream

> 4-inch piece of ginger (to make juice)
> 1 cup raw blanched almonds (skins removed)
> 2 tablespoons maple syrup
> 1 tablespoon vanilla

Pulverize the almonds in a food processor. Grate the ginger and make a ball of it in your palm to squeeze out juice. Add ginger juice, maple syrup, and vanilla to the almonds. To make it creamier you can add a little more pear juice.

Serves 4

Oh, Happy Day Crisp

6 apples
1 quart wild Maine blueberries
4 cups apple juice
6 tablespoons arrowroot
2 teaspoons vanilla
pinch sea salt

Topping

3 cups oats
2 cups barley flour
3/4 cup corn oil or sunflower oil
3/4 cup rice syrup
1 cup chopped walnuts or pecans (I use pecans)
1/4 teaspoon sea salt
1/4 teaspoon cinnamon

Preheat oven to 350 degrees.

Slice the apples and place them in a 9- x 12-inch baking pan with blueberries. Pour the apple juice into a medium saucepan. Dissolve the arrowroot in the cold apple juice, then bring to boil on medium-high heat and let simmer for 2 to 3 minutes. Turn off the heat and add vanilla. To dry roast the oats and barley flour, heat a cast-iron or other skillet on high. Add the oats and flour and stir constantly to prevent burning for 4 to 5 minutes, or until golden.

Heat oil and syrup together and pour over the flour mixture. Add the nuts, cinnamon, and salt. Pour the apple juice mixture over the apples and blueberries. Cover with oat-topping mixture and bake, covered, for 30 minutes. Remove cover and bake for 10 more minutes.

Serves 10–12

Apricot Linzer Cookies

My first encounter with Sanae Suzuki and Eric Lechasseur was through their beautiful cookbooks Love, Eric, and Love, Eric and Sanae. We later met at a Kushi Institute summer conference, where they taught a cooking class on desserts. When my son Francis moved to Los Angeles, he started eating at their Seed Cafe in Venice, California, which has the best vegan macrobiotic food and desserts. Eric, a former French pastry chef, has found a way to create beautiful, delicious desserts that are vegan and sweetened with maple syrup, rice syrup, or juices. Truly healthy. Sanae has an amazing story herself, of healing from ovarian cancer through a macrobiotic diet. It's mentioned in her latest book, Love, Sanae, a boutique cookbook filled with recipes and photographs. It's the most beautiful cookbook I own. Eric has cooked for many celebrities, including Madonna, Tobey Maguire, Sting, Leonardo DiCaprio, and Keenan Ivory Wayans. I'm thrilled that Eric and Sanae shared this recipe.

> 1 cup slivered almonds
> 1 cup rolled oats
> 1 cup whole-grain pastry flour
> $1/2$ teaspoon baking powder
> 1 pinch sea salt
> $1/4$ cup safflower oil
> $1/4$ cup maple syrup
> 1 teaspoon vanilla extract
> 4 ounces unsweetened apricot jam
> powdered coconut (as needed)

Preheat oven to 350 degrees.

In a food processor, process the almonds to a powdered consistency, being careful not to over-mix into an almond butter. Add the oats and process again until lightly coarse.

Add the pastry flour, baking powder, and sea salt. Process for a few seconds and transfer to a bowl.

In a small bowl, whisk the oil, maple syrup, and vanilla. Add the oil mixture to the flour mixture and knead well.

Divide the dough in half. Using a rolling pin, one at a time, roll each dough piece between 2 sheets of parchment paper to form a $1/4$-inch thick rectangle. Peel away the top layer of parchment.

Using a 3- to 4-inch cookie cutter (or a glass), cut the dough into 12 shapes and remove the excess dough. Use a smaller cookie cutter to cut a hole in the center of six of the cookie rounds, leaving the other six intact, and set aside. Repeat the rolling and cutting process with the second half of the dough.

Slide the parchment paper containing the cookies onto a baking sheet and bake for 12 minutes.

Allow the cookies to cool. Spread the jam on the full cookie rounds and place the donut-shaped round on top, making a sandwich. Sprinkle with powdered coconut.

Makes 12 cookies

~~~~~~

Arla's Truffles

An almost-sinfully delicious raw-foods dessert from my daughter Cammie's healthy vegan friend Arla Casselman.

Truffle Coating (make first)
- ¹/₂ **cup Brazil nuts**
- ¹/₂ **cup shredded coconut**

Chop the Brazil nuts and coconut in a food processor. Pour in a bowl and set aside for coating.

Then:
- 1 **cup Brazil nuts**
- ³/₄ **cup walnuts**
- ¹/₈ **cup dates (about 3)**
- ¹/₂ **cup dried apricots**
- 1 or 2 **tablespoons brown rice syrup**
- ¹/₄ **teaspoon vanilla**
- ¹/₂ **cup shredded coconut**
- 2 **tablespoons organic raw cocoa powder (omit if you'd prefer plain)**

Run the Brazil nuts, walnuts, dates, and apricots through the food processor until evenly chopped. Add remaining ingredients and process until combined. Roll into balls, then roll each ball in the coating mixture to finish. Enjoy!

Serves 12–18

Note: These keep best if stored in the refrigerator.

Masao's Blueberry Cake

When I was just starting to improve my diet 11 years ago, I fortuitously discovered Masao Miyaji's wonderful restaurant, Masao's Kitchen, in Waltham, Massachusetts. I appreciate his place so much, not only because I love the food, but also because Masao seems to put love and good energy into the food. Every time I'm anywhere near Boston, I seem to find my way directly to Masao's. When I stop there to eat, I order an extra meal to take home. It's always a big treat. And the recipe below is my favorite treat. One way or another, I figure out a way to get this cake every year for my birthday. For my fiftieth, my husband Tom even drove four hours, down and back, to get it for me! Masao also sells this amazing cake by the slice. Go there and try his food, you will not be disappointed.

Dry Ingredients

> 1 cup organic unbleached all-purpose flour (before sifting)
> 2 1/2 cups organic unbleached pastry flour (before sifting) (You can also use only all-purpose flour—3 1/2 cups)
> 1 teaspoon baking soda (if you use baking powder, use 2 teaspoons instead)
> *optional:* 1 teaspoon cream of tartar

Liquid Ingredients

> 1 1/2 cups organic soy milk
> 3/4 to 1 cup organic maple syrup
> 1/2 to 3/4 cup organic safflower oil
> *optional:* 1/2 teaspoon organic orange extract
> 1/2 teaspoon sea salt
> 1 cup organic wild blueberries (fresh or frozen)

Preheat oven to 325 degrees.

Sift all the dry ingredients together. Mix well all liquid ingredients, then pour into the dry ingredients mixture. Mix until all lumps disappear, but do not over-mix. Mixture should be a little harder than regular pancake mix. You can adjust with extra flour or soy milk to get the right consistency.

Add 1/2 cup of blueberries and mix with a rubber spatula.

Pour mixture into a 9- x 12-inch oblong baking pan and sprinkle the other 1/2 cup of blueberries on top of the mixture. You don't have to oil or line the pan with baking paper because the eggless cake mixture doesn't stick to any kind of baking pans.

Bake for 45 to 50 minutes, until the top of the cake becomes light brown.

Serves 10–12

Optional: Before serving, spread some fruit jam, apple butter, or crushed roasted nuts with a few drops of rice syrup over the cake.

~~~~~~

Koo-Koo for Kuzu Apples

2 apples, washed and sliced (if organic, keep skin on)
1 cup water
1 cup apple juice
pinch of sea salt
2 teaspoons kuzu, diluted in ¼ cup cold water
pinch of cinnamon and/or nutmeg

Add the water and apple juice to a sauce pan with a pinch of salt, begin to heat on medium-high and bring to a boil. Add the apples and reduce heat to low and simmer for 5 to 10 minutes.

In a separate bowl, dilute kuzu in cold water, stirring until it has dissolved with no lumps.

Add the kuzu mixture to the apple juice mixture and stir. Return it to a low boil, then reduce heat to low and continue to simmer for 10 to 15 minutes until the apple softens.

Add optional spices and stir. Serve warm.

Serves 2

Coconut Cookies

I met Warren Kramer back in the fall of 1999, when I'd been practicing macrobiotics for about 10 months. He made me understand that there actually were people out there who could help me fine-tune the diet for my condition. This was incredibly helpful. Warren came up to Maine from Massachusetts a few times a year to teach cooking classes, counsel people, and give lectures, and I looked forward to those visits. In 2006, I met Warren's future wife Fatim, a native of Morocco.

$1/2$ cups whole-wheat pastry flour
1 cup unbleached white flour
generous pinch of sea salt
1 teaspoon baking powder
$1/4$ cup light safflower oil
$1/3$ cup brown rice syrup
$1/3$ to $1/2$ cup Eden Rice Soyblend
1 cup unsweetened shredded coconut
4 tablespoons orange blossom water
$1/2$ cup 100 percent fruit jam

Preheat oven to 350 degrees and line a baking sheet with parchment paper.

Whisk together the flour, salt, and baking powder in a mixing bowl. In another bowl, mix together the oil and rice syrup.

Mix the contents of both bowls together and slowly add enough rice syrup and Soyblend to create a soft pliable dough. Do not over-mix.

With moist hands, roll the dough into 1-inch spheres and arrange about one inch apart on the lined baking sheet. Bake for 15 minutes, until the cookies are golden.

Mix the orange blossom water with the jam, then dip the cookies in this mixture. Roll them in shredded coconut, making sure the coconut sticks to the cookie.

Arrange on a platter and let them sit for at least 30 minutes. The longer the better, as the jam will penetrate into the cookies and make them more delicious.

Makes 18–20 cookies

Warren says: "My mother used to make these cookies for special holidays and make them a day ahead. They were so delicious we couldn't stop eating them!"

Almond Pudding with Berries

When my friend and cooking instructor Lisa Silverman and my husband Tom and I went to the Kushi Institute summer conference in 2009, we brought back handouts of some of the recipes made in the cooking classes. Lisa made this recipe and brought it to my house for a summer potluck. It was a gorgeous presentation! This recipe is from Patricio Garcias De Parede, son of the late Luchi Baranda, my favorite Kushi Institute instructor. Luchi was a little woman with a big heart who loved people, and people loved her, too. She was always bright, cheerful, and upbeat. She told our class, with a big smile and twinkling eyes, "Don't cry about your problems because with tears in your eyes you won't be able to see the solution." She was wonderful and I will always remember her cheerful disposition.

3 cups plain soy milk

3/4 cup rice syrup

1 teaspoon kanten flakes

pinch of sea salt

1 tablespoon kuzu or arrowroot powder, dissolved in a little water

1/4 cup smooth roasted almond butter

4 tablespoons pure maple syrup diluted with a little water

1 cup assorted berries, such as blueberries and raspberries, rinsed

fresh mint for garnish

Place the soy milk, rice syrup, kanten, and salt in a pot. Slowly bring to a boil over medium heat, stirring frequently so that it doesn't burn.

Reduce heat to very low and add diluted kuzu or arrowroot little by little, stirring to prevent lumps. Place the almond butter in a bowl with a little hot soy milk mixture and combine. Add back to pot and cook, while stirring, for 2 to 3 minutes.

Transfer the mixture to individual cups and set aside to cool. Refrigerate a little before serving. Serve with a little maple syrup, berries, and mint.

Serves 5

Good-as-Mom's Apple Pie

Pie Crust

> **3 cups whole-wheat pastry flour**
> **1/2 to 2/3 cup olive oil**
> **1/2 teaspoon sea salt**

Preheat oven to 375 degrees.

Sift the flour and sea salt into a large bowl. Add the oil and mix until the flour resembles bread crumbs.

Add enough flour to form dough. Handle as little as possible to keep it light and flaky. Place the dough in the freezer for about 5 minutes.

Roll out the pastry and place in a lightly oiled pie plate. Bake for 15 minutes. Remove and reduce oven temperature to 350 degrees.

Let the pie shell cool before adding the apple filling. Leftover pastry can be rolled out and cut into shapes with a pastry cutter to decorate the top of the pie.

Filling

> **10 medium apples washed, peeled, and sliced**
> **2 to 3 cups apple juice**
> **pinch of sea salt**
> **1 tablespoon rice syrup**
> **2 tablespoons kuzu, diluted in 1/2 cup cold water**

Place the apples, apple juice, and sea salt in a pot. Bring to a boil on medium heat. Simmer for about 10 minutes or until soft. Place the apples in the pie shell.

Mix the diluted kuzu and rice malt with 1 tablespoon of apple juice. Stir gently until thick. Pour over the apples.

Arrange the pastry shapes on top of the pie. Bake at 350 degrees for 35 minutes. Allow to cool before serving.

Serves 8–10

Tofu Whipped Cream

1 (14-ounce) cake firm tofu
2 tablespoons tahini
1 tablespoon vanilla
6 tablespoons rice syrup

Whip all ingredients together and chill for an hour before using.

Eating Fruit as a Dessert

In transitioning to healthier eating, fruit for dessert in place of junk or other non-nutritive foods high in sugar and chemical additives will help with sugar cravings.

Let fruit take the place of cakes, pies, and other baked goods and candy.

Fresh, organic, and in-season is best, but don't let this deter you if you can't afford or find fresh organic. Frozen is the next best. All fruit is better than sugary processed treats for dessert. Remember that fruit shouldn't take the place of vegetables and is best as a snack or dessert. The whole fruit is better than fruit juice, but some juice is OK. It's a better choice of beverage than non-nutritive, sugary soda, and it can be used as a sweetener in cooked desserts.

about meg wolff

I was a happy 33-year-old wife and the mother of an infant daughter and a 4-year-old son when I was diagnosed with bone cancer in 1990. My left leg was amputated above the knee to stop the cancer. You think you're done with the hard stuff after something like that, right? But eight years later, I was diagnosed with invasive breast cancer.

I had a mastectomy, chemotherapy, and radiation, and still doctors told me to make my peace with God. But, wanting to live, I went another route—instead, I dramatically improved my diet. I'm here today—extremely healthy and enthusiastically sharing what I've learned—because of that decision. Changing my diet saved my life. And it also dramatically improved my life.

Making good choices about food is essential to our health and well being. Food is so important in our culture. I believe people in this country are coming around to a healthier way of thinking about food. It's slow going, but it is happening.

That's very exciting to me because I see improving diet as key to improving many other issues in this country. We're painfully aware of the skyrocketing rates of childhood (and adult) obesity, type II diabetes, heart disease, and cancer. Those problems were far less prevalent when I was growing up in the 1960s and '70s in Westbrook, Maine.

Other social problems today relate to *how* we go about eating, too. In my childhood, most moms stayed home and cooked three meals a day. Dinner, which we called supper, was eaten as a family at home every evening around our table. Most days my brother and sisters and I walked home from school for a big, simple but hearty lunch, too. People weren't rushing out the door skipping breakfast, for the most part. Junk food and fast foods hadn't started permeating our culture yet.

Although I'm a realist, and I don't want to turn back the hands of time, it's my hope that people can examine what worked back then and apply some of it to their lives today. Make sure your kids have healthy school lunch options. Slow down a little, and maybe even have dinner with your family a few times a week!

Everything doesn't have to change at once. Small changes in a better direction matter. A lot. I encourage you to think about that—and to try some of the easy and delicious recipes in this cookbook. My goal is to show people that eating healthy is not hard, and it doesn't require you to give up tasty food that is easy to prepare! If I—a former junk-food diehard—can make it work, so can you!

To learn more, please visit my web site, *www.megwolff.com*, or blog, *www.becoming-whole2.com*, or read *Becoming Whole: The Story of My Complete Recovery from Breast Cancer*, and *Breast Cancer Exposed: The Connection Between Food and Survival*.

acknowledgements

I'm deeply grateful to the late Aveline Kushi. After living through the bombing of Hiroshima and Nagasaki, she dedicated her life to a peaceful world by teaching others about healing through a plant-based diet and lifestyle. She inspired many of my recipes. Thank you to Lisa Silverman for being here in Portland and teaching this way of eating at her Five Seasons Cooking School. This was my first introduction to a diet based on whole grains, beans, and vegetables.

Many thank-yous to my husband Tom for all of his hard work to provide me with the financial support to fuel my passion, not to mention his help in the kitchen, with the laundry, and hauling around my stuff, and for so many times being my "legs."

Thank you to my guest contributors for their delicious recipes, their friendship, and all the hard work they're doing to get this vital information out there about the importance of eating well. I especially want to recognize Kathy Freston, Dr. Neal Barnard, T. Colin Campbell, and Sandy Pukel for being so giving of their resources and time.

Thank you to my editor, co-conspirator, friend, and photographer Patty McCarthy, whose love, direction, and help with anything I need continually encourages and inspires me.

Thank you to Eileen Beasley for her ongoing support; my parents—the late Dolores Bettez DeCoste, for teaching me to "play" with everyone, and the importance of putting love into the food; and my gentle dad, J. Mark DeCoste, for giving me the love of reading, among many other things. Thank you to my mother- and father-in-law, Alice and Charlie Wolff, for their continued support and love. And to Dan and Diane Tardy, who have helped to make my living and cooking space beautiful this year.

You are all truly angels!

And many thanks to Michael Steere at Down East Books for taking a chance on me!

index

recipe contributors

Aisha Memon: Aisha's Oatmeal (p. 22)

Tom Wolff: Tom's Irish Fried Rice (p. 25)

Mark Boucher: Loaded Vegan Lasagna (p. 28)

John Herzog, D.O., osteopathic surgeon: John's Powerhouse Pasta (p. 33)

Sheryl Wolff: Elegant Tofu Polenta (p. 34)

Kathy Freston, author of *Quantum Wellness* and *The One*: Old Bay Tofu Cakes with Cream Horseradish and Creole Mustard Sauce over Shaved Fennel Slaw (p. 42)

Rory Freedman, author of *Skinny Bitch*, *Skinny Bitch in the Kitch*, and *Skinny Bastards*: French Scramble (p. 45)

Liz and Steve Bennett: Garlic Spaghetti (p. 49)

Mary Ledue Paine, owner of The Pepperclub/Good Egg Cafe: Good Egg Cafe Tempeh Hash (p. 51)

Lisa Silverman, healthy foods cooking instructor: Corn Pona Lisa (Black Bean and Corn Bread Casserole) (p. 52)

Jessica Porter, author of *The Hip Chick's Guide to Macrobiotics*: Hip Chick's Hambulghur Helper (p. 54)

Heather Mills, animal rights activist, restaurateur: Rosti for One (p. 64)

Rip Esselstyn, firefighter, triathlete, author of *The Engine 2 Diet*: Raise-the-Roof Sweet Potato–Vegetable Lasagna (p. 68)

Lisa Belisle, M.D.: Beet Slaw with Blueberry Vinaigrette (p. 73)

Colleen Taintor: Colleen's Stir-Fry (p. 79)

Kris Carr, documentary filmmaker (*Crazy Sexy Cancer*): Make-Juice-Not-War Green Juice (p. 82)

Christy Morgan: Broccoli Salad with Creamy Mustard Dressing (p. 83)

Neal Barnard, M.D., president, Physicians Committee for Responsible Medicine: Gazpacho (p. 94)

George & Judith Krassner: George's Tuscan Bean and Bread Hearty Stew (p. 102)

Bart Potenza, vegan restaurant owner: Bart's Long-Life Soup (p. 103)

Sandy Pukel, author of *Grains and Greens on the Deep Blue Sea*: Arame-Stuffed Mushrooms (p. 108)

Aine McAteer, journalist, *Oprah.com* contributor: Sweet Potato and Arame Salad with Asian Style Tartar Sauce (p. 112)

Cammie Wolff: Strawberry Shiitake Salad (p. 118)

Verne Verona, author of *Nature's Cancer-Fighting Foods* and *Macrobiotics for Dummies*: Summer Salad Wrap with Garden Greens and Balsamic Vinaigrette (p. 124)

Laetitia Cerou: Salada de Fenouil à l'orange (p. 126)

John Salley, three-time NBA champion: Slam Dunk Guacamole (p. 130)

John Kozinski: Decadent Popcorn (p. 131)

Eric Lechasseur & Sanae Suzuki, authors of *Love, Eric; Love, Eric and Sanae*; and *Love, Sanae:* Apricot Linzer Cookies (p. 138)

Arla Casselman: Arla's Truffles (p. 139)

Masao Miyaji, owner of Masao's Kitchen: Masao's Blueberry Cake (p. 140)

Warren & Fatim Kramer: Coconut Cookies (p. 142)